A PLACE IN HISTORY

Britain's headline news stories remembered

*John Cobb's Napier Railton leaves the surface of the famous banking during the
500 Miles Race at the Brooklands racing circuit, on 18th September, 1937.*

A PLACE IN HISTORY

Britain's headline news stories remembered

Colin Philpott

AMMONITE
PRESS

First published 2012 by
Ammonite Press
an imprint of AE Publications Ltd,
166 High Street, Lewes, East Sussex, BN7 1XU

Text © Colin Philpott, 2012
Images © as listed on page 248
Copyright © in the work AE Publications Ltd, 2012

ISBN 978-1-90770-869-5

While every effort has been made to obtain permission from the copyright holders for
all material used in this book, the publishers will be pleased to hear from anyone who
has not been appropriately acknowledged, and to make a correction in future reprints.

British Cataloguing in Publication Data. A catalogue record of this book
is available from the British Library.

Editor: Richard Wiles
Project Editor: Ian Penberthy
Designer: Robin Shields
Picture researchers: Hedda Roennevig; Press Assoc

Colour reproduction by GMC Reprograp
Printed and bound in China by 1010 Printing Inte

CONTENTS

FOREWORD

I have been recommending this book to my newsroom colleagues as an antidote to 'tragedy tourism'.

Most news journalists know what it is like to arrive breathless on the scene of some terrible disaster with instructions to crank out a report in double-quick time. In our haste we reach for clichés to describe the area – whether it is a "close-knit community", a "rural idyll", or a "tropical paradise". By the time we are able to slow down enough to take in what makes this particular place distinctive, interest in the story is waning, and the news desk is looking at the hotel bills. The caravan moves on.

This book is about what it leaves behind.

Colin Philpott rightly notes in his Introduction that our opportunities to travel in a virtual way are greater than ever.

I was presenting BBC One's lunchtime news on the day of the Dunblane Massacre (which Colin describes on page 92). Getting information and pictures from rural Perthshire was no easy task in those days, and it was not until we went on the air at 1pm that the full extent of the tragedy emerged. The broadcast was such an intense experience that I felt I had almost been to Dunblane myself.

A decade and a half later I found I could get the same sense of 'being there' as history was made simply by watching the crowds in Tahrir Square, Cairo, while working out on the cross-trainer in my local gym.

But virtual travel can never be a substitute for reporting something in the field. Whenever I return to the scene of a story I have covered I find the experience rewarding – and almost always different.

When I went back to Sarajevo many years after covering the siege there I was completely spooked by the Holiday Inn; the memory of the sniper who used to fire at my camera crew every time we entered or left the building was sharp enough to chill that warm summer's day.

When I look at the Grand Hotel in Brighton, by contrast, the memory of the bomb (page 20) seems as remote as a fairy tale, quite lost in today's normality.

Colin Philpott has written about places that celebrate the past and others that have forgotten it. He also records attempts to cover it up, such as the concreting over of Fred and Rosemary West's home in Gloucester (page 48).

His book reminds us that the past is always alive – and that the news happens to real people in real places, not just on the television you watch in the gym.

Edward Stourton
London, May 2012

Above: The façade of Brighton's Grand Hotel, severely damaged by the IRA bomb that exploded killing five people and injuring 40 others – an attempt to assassinate Prime Minister Margaret Thatcher, who was there to attend the Tory Party conference on 12th October, 1984.

INTRODUCTION

"The poetry of history lies in the quasi-miraculous fact that once, on this earth, once, on this familiar spot of ground, walked other men and women, as actual as we are today, thinking their own thoughts, swayed by their own passions, but now all gone, one generation vanishing into another, gone as utterly as we ourselves shall shortly be gone, like ghosts at cockcrow."

G.M.Trevelyan: An Autobiography and Other Essays (1949)

This book is based on a simple premise – that we are fascinated by places where things happened; that we have a natural curiosity about what existed before in places we visit; that we have a need to walk on the ground where history was made, to see, to touch and to feel it for ourselves.

In an age of instant electronic connection to the rest of the world at the click of a mouse, this need to be rooted in place seems to have increased. In this early part of the 21st century it is possible, in a virtual sense, to be somewhere without being there via the Internet and continuous news channels. However, the popularity of live events and the tendency of people to flock to specific locations when news happens is evidence of our continuing need to be rooted in real places despite, or maybe because of, the virtual world created by technology.

So this journey is all about a sense of place. It's all about the fact that place is important to us. It's all about our fascination with the fact that, wherever you are in the world, you will be living, breathing, feeling and thinking where thousands, probably millions, of other people have done so before you, and others will do so in the future. That fascination is heightened when the spot in question has been a scene of great events – sometimes joyous, sometimes calamitous.

Some of the places on this journey were born to be significant; others had it thrust upon them. In some cases, there will be no trace left of the place in question. In others, it might still exist – possibly even largely in its original form. However, the characteristic that all share is that something happened there; that history was made, that people once flocked to these locations, but do so no more, or not for the same reasons.

Above: A 'tonic for the nation', the Southbank site of the Festival of Britain, viewed from the Embankment on 23rd April, 1951, is illuminated for the first time in readiness for the opening of the event on 3rd May, 1951.

The selection of places is deliberately rather random and does not represent a judgement that these are the most significant. These places are simply one selection from thousands where news was made that could be chosen. Like a news bulletin, this journey includes both the scenes of disasters and tragedies, but also the locations of events of political, cultural, social and sporting significance – as well as the downright quirky. Some places may be well known locally, but not particularly known outside their areas. For a place to be included, there has to be someone still alive in the early part of the 21st century who could remember the events associated with it.

This journey does commemorate places, people and events from the past. But it doesn't assume that the past was always better. It looks at what has happened to those places since they were touched by history.

It provides a look at how the changing use of spaces reflects changes in society, particularly changes in economic circumstances and in leisure time.

Some may argue that this interest can sometimes be voyeuristic or prurient, particularly when it focuses on scenes of disaster and tragedy. Another view is that this is about fascination with, and respect for, places that form an everyday part of our living history. It is perhaps telling, although not deliberate, that there is only one stately home and only one castle on this journey, because this is largely the history of ordinary places touched by extraordinary events. This book represents a belief that these locations are worthy of a place in history.

Colin Philpott
Bradford, March 2012

FIRE
AT THE CRYSTAL PALACE

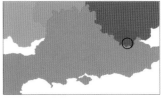

51° 30' 49" N, -0° 9' 24" E

30TH NOVEMBER, 1936   CRYSTAL PALACE PARADE, SYDENHAM, LONDON, SE20 8DT

Alongside what is now a busy but unremarkable suburban thoroughfare in South-east London is the site of one of the most remarkable buildings bequeathed to 20th-century Britain by Victorian Britain.

It is hard to think of a place where – even 75 years and more since it was destroyed in one of the most spectacular peacetime fires in Britain – the ghosts of a building live on so powerfully. It's also hard to think of a place whose story is a better encapsulation of changing use of leisure time from the 19th-, through the 20th- and into the 21st-century.

The Crystal Palace was originally built in Hyde Park in central London for the Great Exhibition of 1851, and envisaged as a temporary structure. After the exhibition ended, the palace was disassembled and rebuilt (on a larger scale) on a hillside at Sydenham in South London, set in a large area of parkland.

The scale of The Crystal Palace was vast. It was more than 1,600 feet long (almost a third of a mile); the total area of the main building was over 600,000 square feet and the total amount of glass surface area was around 1.6m square feet. Its grounds were extensive and included a football ground where the FA Cup Final was played from 1895 to 1914.

It was a multi-purpose leisure venue before anyone had dreamt up such a term. As well as its permanent displays, the variety of the events staged there was astonishing. It

included spectacular Brocks firework displays; a range of concerts, including brass band competitions and concerts involving the magnificent organ in the Palace's great hall, scout jamborees, cat and dog shows, and much more besides. The single most spectacular event held there was the Festival of Empire of 1911, which marked the coronation of King George V. Small-scale replicas of famous buildings from the countries of the British Empire were built in the grounds.

In a way, the Festival of Empire represented the high point of the Palace's fortunes. After that it went into decline and it was declared bankrupt in 1911, but was saved for the nation after a public appeal in 1913. After use as a naval training establishment in the First World War, it reopened in 1920 as the first home of the Imperial War Museum. However, in its last decade, its fortunes had started to improve under the leadership of Sir Henry Buckland and his more populist approach, and the Palace had returned to profit.

DISASTER!

However, just before 7pm on the evening of Monday 30th November, 1936, the Palace staged its most spectacular – and last – display. Sir Henry Buckland was walking along Crystal Palace Parade with his daughter, Chrystal, when they spotted a small glow inside the main transept. Staff were attempting to put out a fire, but without success. With wooden floors and a glass structure, and fanned by strong winds, the Palace fire spread rapidly.

A total of 89 fire engines and more than 400 firemen fought the blaze, which could be seen in eight counties. More than 100,000 people are thought to have converged on the area to watch the fire. By the following morning, the Palace was in ruins. Since then, various theories have been put forward about the cause of the fire, but the most probable explanation is the rather prosaic one that a discarded cigarette under the floor was the likely cause.

Chrystal recalled later: "I couldn't believe how quickly the fire spread and the heat was tremendous. I will never forget the sight of my father the following day standing in the rubble with tears streaming down his face surveying the wreckage of 20 years' work".

By coincidence, the first public television service in Britain provided by the BBC had started exactly four weeks before the fire. The abdication of Edward VIII came 11 days after the fire. These three events together somehow seem, with hindsight, to represent the passing of one age and the beginning of another.

The building was under-insured and fighting talk of rebuilding was overtaken by the advent of the Second

A VICTORIAN PLEASURE PALACE, A SPECTACULAR FIRE, AND A FORLORN PARK

Left: The Hon. Mrs A. Cooper, reflected in the water, casts a salmon fly for distance in the British Bait Casting Tournament, held at The Crystal Palace, on 6th July, 1935.

Below: Imogen Smith, aged eight, poses with a replica Iguanodon at Crystal Palace Park, London, in December 2011. The dinosaur and prehistoric animal park containing 29 life-size statues was restored to its former glory almost 150 years after it was first built.

Above: The ornate Italian Terraces in front of The Crystal Palace were still largely intact after the blaze, and survive now as Listed Grade II structures.

World War. Its twin water towers left standing after the fire (inside one of which John Logie Baird had carried out his early tests for television) were blown up during the war, allegedly because they might be helpful landmarks for German bombers.

REGENERATION

Since the war, the area where the Palace stood has been a caravan site and for a while there was a car racing circuit there. Today, it is incorporated into the wider parkland, where there are signs of what once stood here. The remains of the terracing are still intact and, on the far side of Crystal Palace Parade, there is now a housing development on the site of where The Crystal Palace High-Level Railway Station (closed in 1954) once stood. However, the tunnels that linked the station to the Palace underneath Crystal Palace Parade are still visible.

The grounds include The Crystal Palace National Sports Centre (built on the site of the football stadium). Over the years, a variety of schemes for redeveloping the site (including several that involved some sort of rebuilding of the palace) have come and gone. The area was earmarked in the 1950s and 1960s for the National Exhibition Centre, but it was eventually built near Birmingham instead. The memory of the Victorian structure is preserved by a group of enthusiasts who run the Crystal Palace Museum on the site.

The Crystal Palace was a classic product of the Victorian era – grand, slightly garish, but very functional. It was a place for mass leisure entertainment at a time when the development of the railways made travel possible, even for the poorer sections of society. The Palace flourished for half a century, but the arrival of other means of entertainment – notably cinema and radio – meant its appeal waned. Just as it was starting to find a new role in the 1930s, it was destroyed. Had the fire not happened, and had it survived the Second World War, could it have found a future in the leisure pursuits of 1950s Britain and beyond?

ORPINGTON
V2 FINALE

27TH MARCH, 1945   88 KYNASTON ROAD, ORPINGTON, GREATER LONDON, BR5 4JZ

SCENE OF THE LAST BRITISH CIVILIAN DEATH BY ENEMY ACTION IN THE SECOND WORLD WAR

Above: Aerial attack: a V2 rocket in the process of being elevated into the vertical firing position in Cuxhaven, Germany, in October 1945.

On a pleasant spring afternoon with the end of the Second World War in sight, Ivy Millichamp was in the kitchen of her home – a comfortable bungalow in the London suburb of Orpington – when a German V2 rocket landed in her street. She took the full force of the blast, and when her husband, Eric, pulled her from the wreckage of their house, she was already dead.

A total of 24 people were injured in the attack, including several of Ivy's neighbours at numbers 82, 84 and 86, and people in nearby Court Road, but, remarkably, Ivy was the only fatality. In death she acquired a rather macabre form of celebrity – she was the last civilian to be killed by enemy action on British soil in the Second World War. Her death came less than six weeks before the war in Europe ended in early May of 1945.

The V2 rocket that killed Ivy Millichamp had been launched by retreating German forces from Holland as a last act of defiance as Allied armies advanced towards the rocket launching sites. On that day in March, two V2s were launched. The first was aimed at Antwerp, Belgium, where it landed killing 27 people; the second fell short of its target of central London, landing in Orpington. They were to be the last V2 rockets fired, although there were further V1 attacks on the two following days but with no further loss of life.

FLYING BOMB

The first 'secret weapon' of the Nazis in their last desperate attempt to reverse the tide of the war was the V1 (known as the doodlebug), which terrorised South East England from 1944. They had a distinctive droning noise and many were shot down. However, the V2 flying bomb was deadlier because it could not be spotted in advance or shot down. More than 5,000 were launched at Britain. Only around 1,100 reached these shores but more than 2,500 people were killed by V2s.

The probable reason for the last V2 landing in Orpington was the result of some double-cross intelligence by the British secret services. The British were able to infiltrate German intelligence networks and send false information suggesting that V2s were overshooting their target of central London. This is thought to have led to a recalibration of the trajectory of the V2s by the Germans, which meant that many V2s subsequently landed short of central London. In many cases – although not in this one – V2s landed harmlessly in the Kentish countryside as a result of this ruse by British intelligence.

Ivy Millichamp, who was 34 when she was killed, was originally from Essex. She married Eric in 1938 and they moved to Orpington to be close to Eric's work. Only two months before the attack, a V1 bomb had landed in Court Road, close to their home, killing eight people.

Ivy was buried in the nearby All Saints Churchyard on 3rd April, 1945, in an unmarked grave. More than 40 years later, a headstone was erected to mark her grave.

Despite the austerity of immediate post-war Britain, the bungalows severely damaged in Kynaston Road were swiftly rebuilt. Now you would never guess as you walk down the street that such carnage had been wrought in this residential backwater.

Above: The severely damaged bungalows in Kynaston Road, Orpington.
Below left: The former Millichamp home, rebuilt after the V2 attack.
Below right: Ivy Millichamp, who died in the rocket attack.

WRECK OF
HMS BULWARK

51° 25' 11" N, 0° 33' 44" E

26TH NOVEMBER, 1914

KETHOLE REACH, NEAR SHEERNESS, KENT, ME3 9LD

MORE THAN 700 DEAD IN A MUNITIONS EXPLOSION ABOARD A BATTLESHIP

On the morning of Thursday, 26th November, 1914, the crew of the British battleship HMS *Bulwark* were going about their normal routine, while moored in the estuary of the River Medway about four miles west of Sheerness on the Isle of Sheppey in Kent. The ship's band was rehearsing, some crew were practising their drill and others were eating breakfast. It was just three months into the First World War and the battleship had been moved to the Kent coast, along with other ships of the fleet, to guard against a possible German invasion.

At around 7.50am a rumbling sound was heard

before a huge sheet of flame and debris shot into the air. A thick cloud of smoke appeared and, when it had cleared, the ship had sunk without trace. The explosion was heard 20 miles away in Whitstable and across the Thames Estuary on the Essex coast, where Southend Pier was said to have been shaken by the force of the blast.

Neighbouring ships went to the assistance of the *Bulwark,* but there were only 12 survivors from the explosion. A total of 738 officers and crew had perished in what remains the worst naval disaster in terms of loss of life in England.

Rumours abounded in the immediate aftermath of the explosion. Some nearby residents assumed that the feared Zeppelin raids had begun. A naval Court of Inquiry was established two days later and it discovered that the practice had been to store the *Bulwark's* supply of shells in cross passageways between the ship's magazines. It concluded that the likely cause of the explosion was overheated cordite charges, which set off a series of explosions.

TRAGIC ACCIDENT

The wreck of the *Bulwark* is officially designated a war grave. The ship, which was blown apart into several sections, lies in the estuary between Sheerness and the Kingsnorth Power Station. A memorial to those who died was erected at the dockyard church in Sheerness. Many of the victims of the disaster were never recovered, but some are buried at Woodlands Cemetery in Gillingham, Kent.

On 27th May the following year, Sheerness witnessed another naval tragedy when the minesweeper, HMS *Princess Irene*, blew up in a similarly spectacular explosion with the loss of 352 lives. The coincidence of two explosions in the same area within six months of each other led to suspicions of sabotage, and a worker at Chatham Dockyard was named as a suspect, although he was cleared after an investigation by Special Branch.

The ghosts of the area's naval past still hang in the air in and around the Isle of Sheppey and the Medway Estuary. There are numerous wrecks in the area and the naval tradition of this part of the country is commemorated at the Historic Dockyard, Chatham, which closed in 1984 and became a museum and visitor attraction.

Above: The Portsmouth Naval Memorial, Southsea, Hampshire, which commemorates sailors who died at sea during the First and Second World Wars, including victims from HMS Bulwark.

Facing page: The Formidable-Class *battleship, HMS* Bulwark, *launched on 18th October, 1899, is shown less than four months before the tragic explosion that killed more than 700 of her crew.*

DOVER'S WARTIME COMMAND CENTRE

51° 7' 44" N, 1° 19' 6" E

27TH MAY–4TH JUNE, 1940

DOVER CASTLE, DOVER, KENT, CT16 1HU

TUNNELS WHERE THE EVACUATION OF DUNKIRK WAS MASTERMINDED

Left: Three months after Operation Dynamo, the Dunkirk evacuation, Sir Winston Churchill and Vice-Admiral Sir Bertram Ramsay inspect maps at Naval HQ in tunnels beneath Dover Castle, on 28th August, 1940.

Most of the places visited on this journey have not been turned into visitor attractions. Indeed, that is part of their appeal – they bear witness to the memorable events that took place there modestly or, in many cases, silently. However, Dover Castle's contribution to the defence of Britain in general, and its specific contribution to the war effort during the Second World War, has been commemorated with a full-on visitor experience. Nevertheless, this journey has to

pass by here because of the events of a single week in May–June, 1940, that have done so much to shape the British psyche since.

The phrase "The Dunkirk Spirit" resonates down the years and is still brought out well into the 21st century to denote examples of people pulling together in times of adversity. The basic facts of the Dunkirk evacuation are well known. Nine months into the Second World War, the British Expeditionary Force fighting in France was cut off and surrounded by the advancing German forces near the port of Dunkirk on the French coast. A fleet of ships, naval and civilian, was assembled to rescue them from the harbour and off the beaches at Dunkirk.

In the period between 27th May and 4th June, 1940 a total of more than 338,000 service personnel, French as well as British soldiers, were plucked from Dunkirk, despite an aerial bombardment by the German Luftwaffe, and brought back to Britain. Enormous quantities of equipment were lost at Dunkirk and many men were killed or captured by the Germans. Despite the losses, the evacuation of Dunkirk was hailed a success. A large proportion of Britain's fighting force was kept intact and the operation was a psychological boost.

STRATEGIC ROLE

The Dunkirk evacuation was masterminded from a command centre across the channel in the tunnels dug into the cliffs below Dover Castle on the Kent coast. The tunnels had been built at the time of the Napoleonic Wars to provide barracks as Dover expanded its role as a garrison town. More than 2,000 troops were accommodated there at the beginning of the 19th century. From 1826, they lay unused and abandoned until the outbreak of the Second World War.

In September 1939 Vice-Admiral Sir Bertram Ramsay was given a space within one of the six tunnels in which to set up his military command, alongside the Castle's garrison. It was from here that the Dunkirk evacuation was planned and overseen. This highlighted Dover's strategic importance and later in the war two more sets of tunnels were built, one as a military hospital, and another as a CHQ (combined military headquarters). Later in 1944, the Dover tunnels played another crucial role as a command centre for the D-Day landings.

After the War, the tunnels were earmarked as a Regional Centre of Government in the event of a nuclear war. They were in the process of being upgraded in the 1980s when government policy changed as the Cold War came to an end with the fall of the Soviet Union. Instead, the tunnels were handed over to English Heritage to open to the public in recognition of the key role this place played in the course of the Second World War.

Right and below: A recreation of the Coastal Artillery Operations Room in the tunnels beneath Dover Castle is part of a permanent exhibition 'Operation Dynamo: Rescue from Dunkirk'.

Bottom right: Former Dover Castle Artillery Operations Room employees, (L–R) Wynn Wakefield, May Owen and Pam Pettit at the plotting table used to mastermind the naval defence of the Kent coastline during the Second World War, in the English Heritage War Room.

GRAND HOTEL
BRIGHTON BOMBING

50° 49' 17" N, -0° 8' 50" E

12TH OCTOBER, 1984　　　　GRAND HOTEL, 97–99 KINGS ROAD, BRIGHTON, EAST SUSSEX, BN1 2FW

SCENE OF THE ATTEMPTED
ASSASSINATION OF THE BRITISH
PRIME MINISTER

Left: Prime Minister Margaret Thatcher and her husband Denis leaving the Royal Sussex County Hospital in Brighton after visiting the victims of the IRA bomb explosion that occurred at the hotel in which she was staying.

Facing page: Severe damage was caused to the exterior of the Grand Hotel, Brighton, when the IRA bomb exploded in a sixth floor bathroom.

The sight of the then Conservative Cabinet Minister, Norman Tebbit, in his pyjamas, being pulled from the wreckage of the Grand Hotel in Brighton on an autumn morning in 1984 is one of the most enduring British news images of the late 20th century. The events of Friday, 12th October of that year – the last day of the Conservative Party Conference in Brighton, East Sussex – represent the highpoint of Irish Republican terrorism on the British mainland during the 1970s and 1980s. This was, by some way, the most dramatic act of the IRA in pursuit of their goal of a united Ireland – an attempt to kill the British Prime Minister.

When the bomb exploded on the sixth floor just before three o'clock that morning, Margaret Thatcher was still up working on her closing day conference speech. The blast ripped through the bathroom of her suite on the first floor but her bedroom and living room were unaffected. Thatcher – Britain's first woman prime minister and a figure who provoked admiration and hatred in equal measures – was uninjured. Five people died in the explosion, including a Conservative MP, Sir Anthony Berry, and Roberta Wakeham – the wife of the Chief Whip,

John Wakeham. The three others who died were Muriel Maclean, wife of the Leader of the Scottish Conservatives; Eric Taylor, who was Chairman of the North-West Area Conservatives; and Jeanne Shattock, wife of the President of the South West Conservative Association. More than 40 people were injured, including several who were permanently disabled – among them, Norman Tebbit's wife, Margaret.

Margaret Thatcher famously insisted that the conference should carry on and she delivered her speech as planned later that morning in which she declared that terrorism would never succeed.

BOMBER FREED

Patrick Magee was convicted of the bombing in 1986 and given seven life sentences. Magee, who was born in Belfast but brought up in England, had been involved in the IRA since returning to Northern Ireland as an adult. Magee had apparently checked into the hotel under a false name about three weeks before the explosion and placed the bomb with a timer under the bath in his room. Magee was released in 1999 as a consequence

Left: The shattered top four floors of the Grand Hotel after the IRA bomb, planted by Patrick Magee, had injured more than 40 people and killed five.

of the Good Friday Peace Agreement in Northern Ireland. His release provoked enormous controversy. He subsequently expressed regret for innocent lives lost in the bombing. Magee met Jo Berry, the daughter of Sir Anthony Berry, killed in the bombing, several times after his release, and a BBC programme in 2001 featured their meetings and discussions. Magee has continued to support Irish republicanism, but has been involved in a number of reconciliation initiatives.

ICON RESTORED

The Grand Hotel, which had been built originally in 1864, was shut for nearly two years following the bombing and reopened on 28th August, 1986 in a ceremony attended by Margaret Thatcher and Norman Tebbit. The man who oversaw the £19m rebuild of the hotel was Richard Baker, who had been appointed to the job of general manager just a few months before the bombing, but had yet to take up the role. The rebuilding restored the hotel almost exactly to its former state and the bedrooms destroyed in the explosion were all replaced, although in a modified way. The location where the bomb was planted is now Room 621.

Since 1986 the Grand has resumed its role as one of the icons of the English seaside – a Victorian hotel recalling the splendours of an earlier age. The events of October 1984 are remembered in the hotel with a plaque that was unveiled on the 25th anniversary and a montage of newspaper cuttings.

Above: Prime Minister Margaret Thatcher insisted on giving a speech at the Conservative Party Conference in Brighton, despite the bomb blast that was intended to assassinate her earlier the same morning.

Below: The opulent Grand Hotel – now something of an icon in the seaside town – was restored to its former glory, positioned at the centre of the famous seafront.

Above: Lord Tebbit unveils a plaque at the Grand Hotel to mark the 25th anniversary of the bombing, on 12th October, 2009.

BRIGHTON'S DERELICT
WEST PIER

50° 49' 17" N, -0° 9' 2" E

1866–1975

KING'S ROAD, BRIGHTON, EAST SUSSEX, BN1 2FL

FORLORN HULK OF A PIER REFUSING TO DIE

Above: An aerial photograph of the West Pier from the mid-20th century shows the structure in its final form, before it succumbed to the effects of storm and fire.

Above: West Pier in 1929 was a popular and fashionable venue. In 1916 a large concert hall had been erected in the central part of the pier, and it also featured a bandstand and steamer landing stages.

Above: A woman gazes out on the rusting shell of West Pier. It had been cut off from the shore since the early 1990s, but a partial collapse occurred during a storm in 2002, and a fire in 2003 destroyed the pavilion at the end.

Standing on Brighton beach it's sometimes difficult to understand how a rusting hulk of metal a few hundred yards out to sea can generate such passion and such controversy. Yet Brighton's West Pier – or rather the sad remains of it – has certainly done that over the years and continues to do so.

Originally, many piers were built for a practical purpose to allow visiting ships to dock, but they were developed into multi-purpose entertainment venues protruding out over the sea. Others, like the West Pier, were built as pleasure piers from the start. Perhaps astonishingly, almost 60 piers remain around the British coast, although around 40 others have been lost. Some have been battered by the sea. Many have succumbed to fire – sometimes arson.

PIER PRESSURE

Brighton West Pier was opened in 1866. Originally, it was a simple structure with six ornamental houses built on it, but it was transformed over the years with a concert hall, pier head and other features added. Its heyday was between the wars and into the 1950s. During the 1920s, the pier was very popular. Its attractions included paddle steamer excursions from the pier, military bands, diving and bathing from the pier head, as well as a resident orchestra and a year-round programme in the theatre. By the 1950s, the pier had changed and it had more of the feel of the funfair, with a helter skelter, dodgems, a ghost train and miniature track racing – but it was still thriving. Thereafter, a slow decline ensued as British seaside resorts suffered from foreign competition and the West Pier specifically competed with its local rival, the Palace Pier, only 1,000 yards to the east. New owners attempted a revival in the 1960s but in 1975 it was closed.

AMBITIOUS PLANS

Since then the story of the West Pier has been a long running saga of hope and disappointment in equal measure. A series of storms and fires have reduced the pier to a metal rump stuck out incongruously a few hundred yards from the shore. The West Pier Trust, established to protect it, remains optimistic about its aim of building a new pier. The Trust hopes this could follow on from the development of the i360 – a 575-feet high observation tower planned for the landward end.

There are many who oppose redevelopment and the West Pier, a Grade One listed structure, remains a subject that divides opinion among the people of Brighton.

PORTSMOUTH'S
TRICORN
CENTRE

1966–2004

50° 48' 6" N, 1° 5' 23" W

Above: Premium shops stayed away and market traders shunned the dark, dank atmosphere of the centre.

SITE OF FORMER 1960s SHOPPING CENTRE
ONCE VOTED BRITAIN'S UGLIEST BUILDING

In many ways, Portsmouth's Tricorn Centre symbolises the 1960s. It was a very ordinary place where people did ordinary things. People parked their cars; they shopped; some went to the nightclub; a few even lived there in one of the eight flats built as part of the development. However,

it represents an important development in city centre architecture and planning from the 1960s, and it is now much loved and missed by many who mourned its eventual demolition in 2004.

The Tricorn Centre was designed by Owen Luder and Rodney Gordon, who created a multi-layered building

Above: Concrete jungle. Graffiti defaces the bleak façade. Portsmouth's wet coastal climate caused structural steel within the concrete to rust, causing expansion of the concrete; small stalactites grew off ledges.

Above: Brutal treatment? In early March 2004 the government refused permission to grant the dilapidated Tricorn Centre listed buildings status, thus sealing its fate.

for multiple uses. There were shops, pubs, a petrol station and a public square on the ground floor, a market on the first floor and then a nightclub, a Laser Quest facility and flats higher up with car parking on seven storeys. Later in its history there was a casino.

BRUTALIST

The Tricorn, opened in 1966 and seen as representative of the so-called 'Brutalist' school of architecture, was something of a forerunner for other developments, including the Barbican in London. It had been part of an attempt to revitalise Portsmouth but, from the start, it struggled. It was away from the main centre of the city and never attracted the major shops. A Fine Fare supermarket was the high point of its retail offer.

During its 38-year history, the Tricorn acquired an unenviable accolade – it was frequently chosen among Britain's ugliest buildings and, in a BBC poll in 2001, it was voted the most hated building in Britain.

DISMAL REPUTATION

By 2002, all the shops had gone and the Tricorn lived on for a couple of years as a car park. It was said to be a favourite suicide spot because it was one of the tallest publicly accessible buildings in the area. Despite its unpopularity with some people, there were attempts, which proved unsuccessful, to get the building listed as an example of 1960s architecture.

Since its demolition in 2004, it has served as a ground level car park, while ambitious plans have been developed for a new Northern Quarter on the site, with higher-class retailers than the Tricorn managed to attract. By 2012, these plans were yet to come to fruition. Nevertheless, the Tricorn is held in affection by many people and there are plans to mark the tenth anniversary of its disappearance in 2014.

Above: Demolition begins at 'Britain's ugliest building', after a ceremony held by Portsmouth City Council to celebrate the demise of the building, which critics said had blighted the area since it was built in 1966.

ISLE OF WIGHT
FESTIVAL '69

50° 43' 47" N, 1° 14' 2" W

29TH–31ST AUGUST, 1969　　　　WOODSIDE BAY, WOOTTON BRIDGE, ISLE OF WIGHT, PO33 4PZ

BOB DYLAN APPEARS ON A HILLSIDE ON THE ISLE OF WIGHT

What happened in the tiny village of Wootton on the Isle of Wight on the weekend of 29th, 30th and 31st August, 1969 is the stuff of legends. In what was then, and more than 40 years on was still, a field overlooking the northern coastline of a generally sleepy island, perhaps the greatest rock musician of his age appeared in front of at least 100,000 people.

It was the most unlikely booking in the most unlikely setting. Bob Dylan had been expected to appear at the Woodstock Festival, which had taken place a couple of weeks earlier in upstate New York, not far from his home. He turned down the invitation and set sail for Britain on the very day Woodstock started. A variety of reasons have been advanced over the years to explain why the rock legend chose Wight over Woodstock, but choose he did.

What may have helped was the rumoured $50,000 (around £250,000 at 2012 values) that the promoters had offered Dylan. The festival was the brainchild of Ray, Ron and Bill Foulk, all in their early twenties, assisted by the rock promoter Rikki Farr. They searched the island for potential sites and eventually secured planning permission for fields to the north of the village of Wootton Bridge, not far from the ferry connection to the mainland at Ryde.

They then scoured the music industry for talent and were able to persuade some of the leading bands of the

Far left: The colourful festival programme has become a collector's item in the 21st century.
Left: Bob Dylan chats to members of the press on his arrival in the Isle of Wight.

Above: Dylan and the festival promoters hold a press conference. The Foulk brothers had successfully tempted the rock legend to their Isle of Wight festival over Woodstock.

Right: Music fans savour the ambience of the festival and its impressive line-up.

time to assemble in a remote corner of an island not normally associated with the rock music scene. The line up included the Bonzo Dog Doo-dah Band, Tom Paxton, Joe Cocker and The Who.

STAR TURN

The high point of the festival came after 11 o'clock on the Sunday night, when Dylan finally appeared. It was his first live appearance for three years after a motorcycle accident. He played 17 numbers in front of probably the biggest audience of his career. Those who attended the Dylan performance are said to have included three of The Beatles, Jane Fonda, Eric Clapton, Keith Richards and Elton John. When he finished, the crowds filed away down the narrow country lanes.

The festival was deemed a success. It passed off without any real trouble, despite the fact that it effectively doubled, or even trebled, the island's population of 100,000 for a weekend. Some estimates put the total attendance at over 300,000, although it's thought that there were somewhere between 100,000 and 150,000 there on the Sunday night when Dylan played. Forty years on, local people now recall the event with some affection, although they do remember that the village was unprepared to deal with the influx of

people – particularly in the provision of toilets.

The 1969 Isle of Wight Festival was the second of three such festivals held on the island in successive years. All three remain seared into the collective folklore of rock music. The first, in 1968, had been a much smaller event, held at Ford Farm near Godshill in the south of the island, with Jefferson Airplane as the headline guest. Around 10,000 people are thought to have attended.

In 1970, buoyed by the success of the 1969 event, the organisers thought big. The festival was held at Afton Down, near Freshwater and is rumoured to have attracted up to 600,000 people. The line-up was arguably even more impressive. It included The Who, Joan Baez, Jethro Tull, the Moody Blues and Jimi Hendrix (just a few weeks before his death).

In 2002 the Isle of Wight Festival was revived and has been held annually since, but not at any of the original sites. More than 40 years later, websites dedicated to the memory of the original Isle of Wight Festivals still flourish and still attract fresh material. All three festival sites returned to their original agricultural use but the memories created there live on and form part of the warm glow that still surrounds the late 1960s.

Facing page: An aerial photograph shows a mass of up to 200,000 fans gathered for the Isle of Wight Festival.

Right: Distinctive graphics publicised the Festival in true Sixties fashion.

Below: Jo Boyden, 18, of Dorset, peers from her hut built from paper sacks, straw and odd timber at the Isle of Wight Festival.

Below right: A young festival-goer is ferried across the sea of fans in a Moses basket.

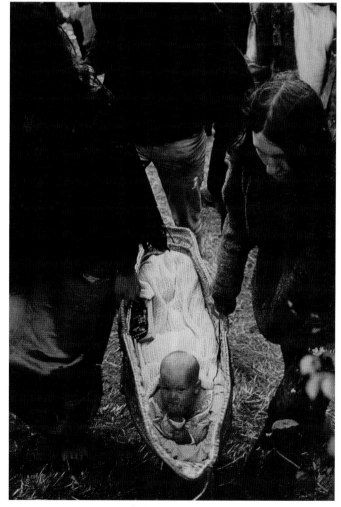

IMBER
VILLAGE

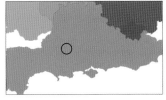

51° 17' 3" N, 2° 0' 50" W

1ST NOVEMBER, 1943   IMBER VILLAGE, WEST OF THE A360, SALISBURY PLAIN, WILTSHIRE, SN10 4JY

AN ABANDONED VILLAGE TAKEN OVER BY THE MILITARY

Left: The windowless shell of the old post office in the village of Imber, which was requisitioned by the military in 1943.

Above: An ominous warning deters sightseers from approaching the buildings constructed by the military for use in training.

On 1st November, 1943 the villagers of Imber, Wiltshire, were called to a meeting at which they were given 47 days notice to vacate their homes. The military wanted the village so that American troops could practise street fighting, in advance of the Allied invasion of France. Most of the 150 or so villagers put up little or no resistance to eviction from their homes, believing that it was their contribution to the war effort. The villagers, who were given some compensation, were apparently led to believe that they would be able to return to their homes in the future. However, almost 70 years on, this had never happened, and the village is still in the control of the military and used for training.

In fact, the Army had been acquiring land on Salisbury Plain for many years prior to the Second World War. Much of the land in and around Imber had already been bought up before 1943. A depression in the farming business and the attractive prices the Army were offering had previously persuaded landowners to sell to the military.

Above: Damage to the wall and chimney stack of this terrace of 1938 houses was, the War Office claimed in 1948, due to faulty ammunition, since Imber had not been deliberately used as a target.

Above: A notice warning soldiers of the boundaries of Imber is read by a soldier beside a crumbling wall in the deserted village, in April 1948.

Left: The rural charm of Domesday village Imber, seen in 1948, conceals a more sinister fact. It's here that soldiers are schooled in the tactics of street fighting.

STREET FIGHTING

Since the Second World War the Army has used the village to simulate street fighting. It is believed that Imber was used to train troops for service in Northern Ireland and, more recently, for duty in Iraq. Over the years the military acquired more property in the village, taking over the pub and other buildings. They have also built modern houses there for use in training. The only building not owned by the military is St Giles Church, which had fallen into disrepair but was restored between 2008 and 2009.

In 1961, more than 2,000 people attended a rally to campaign for villagers to be allowed to return. A public inquiry was held to consider the matter, but this ruled in favour of continued military use. In the early 1970s, a further unsuccessful attempt was made despite the emergence of written evidence from the 1940s promising that villagers would be able to return to their homes.

It is possible to gain access to Imber at certain times of the year. There is an annual carol service in St Giles just before Christmas and there are open days on a number of occasions each year.

CARDIFF
ARMS PARK

51° 28' 46" N, 3° 11' 1" W

WESTGATE STREET, CARDIFF, WALES, CF10 1JA

THE GREATEST TRY IN THE HISTORY OF RUGBY AT THE GREATEST STADIUM?

In the run up to the famous try, the Barbarians' Tom David (above left) passes the ball to Derrick Quinnell (out of picture), while being felled by New Zealand's J.F. Karam, then (above) Barbarians' Gareth Edwards (centre) passes inside, and then (left) passes to the wing.

Sports fans are perhaps over-fond of waxing lyrical about the quasi-spiritual experience of being part of a crowd, and they are perhaps too quick to describe the stadia where their teams play as 'cathedrals' or 'theatres of dreams'. However, there were few experiences more guaranteed to make the hairs on the back of your neck stand on end than being part of the crowd singing *Land of My Fathers* at the ancestral home of Welsh rugby, the Arms Park in Cardiff. Somehow the Arms Park exerted, and still exerts, a particular hold over the imagination that only a handful of sports stadia ever quite achieve.

Maybe, for people of a certain age, whether or not they are Welsh, it is the memory of Gareth Edwards, Barry John and J.P.R. Williams from the 1960s and 1970s playing rugby with great passion and fervour on murky winter days, captured by grainy film and TV coverage. The bringing together of two great Welsh traditions, rugby and singing, in a cauldron of noise and passion is why the Arms Park still holds a fascination for many well beyond the borders of the Principality.

FAST ACTION

Many great games were played at the Arms Park, but the one that encapsulates the spirit of the place was not, in fact, a Welsh national match but a game between the Barbarians (the ad-hoc British team that combines the talents of the English, Welsh, Scottish and Irish) and the New Zealand All-Blacks, on 27th January, 1973. For many years during the 20th century a traditional climax of a tour of the British Isles by the New Zealand, Australian or South African rugby teams was a game against the 'Baa-Baas'. The game in 1973 was fast and furious, and the Barbarians eventually won 23–11. It is best remembered for a glorious try by the

Above: Cardiff Arms Park during the Five Nations Championship between Wales and Ireland on 12th March, 1932.

Above: The short-lived National Stadium, in February 1996, was built during the 1970s and 1980s, but demolished after only a decade.

Above: In November 1997, a new landmark rises in Cardiff from the demolished home of Welsh rugby, as the Millennium Stadium takes shape.

Above: The new Millennium stadium, viewed in January 1999, was built directly behind the old Cardiff RFC ground.

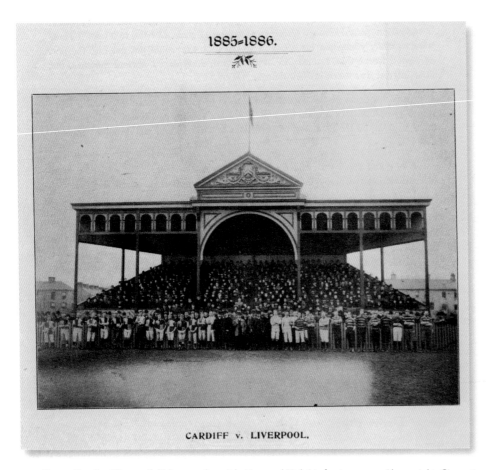

1885-1886.

CARDIFF v. LIVERPOOL.

OGDEN'S CIGARETTES.

CARDIFF.

Above: The Cardiff team (left) line up alongside Liverpool (right) in front of the new stand at the Arms Park, Boxing Day 1885. Cardiff won by three goals and one minor (unconverted try) to one minor.

Above right: Cigarette cards, used to stiffen packaging and advertise brands, typically bore the likenesses of sportsmen, such as this Welsh rugby player from 1906.

Welshman, Gareth Edwards, which was the culmination of a move from the far end of the pitch without any All-Blacks players touching the ball.

UNDER DEVELOPMENT

The story of the stadia that have existed on the Arms Park site is a complicated one. In effect four different stadia have existed where the 1973 Barbarians–All-Blacks match and many other iconic rugby moments took place. The first was established in the 1880s when both a rugby ground and a cricket ground (the home of Glamorgan Cricket Club) were built. The Arms Park was progressively developed during the first half of the 20th century, including a new South Stand opened in time

for the Empire and Commonwealth Games, which were held in Wales in 1958.

By then the capacity of the rugby stadium had risen to 60,000. However, a debate was underway about the future of the whole complex partly sparked off by serious flooding of the stadium in 1960, when the River Taff broke its banks. In the end, the decision was taken to relocate the cricket ground away from the Arms Park and Glamorgan County Cricket Club moved to Sophia Gardens – about a mile away in Cardiff – in 1967.

Two new rugby grounds were then built on the site – a new National Stadium for the Welsh national team and a new ground (on part of the site of the old cricket ground) for Cardiff RFC. The building of the new stands took place progressively in the 1970s and 1980s and the new National Stadium was officially opened in April 1984.

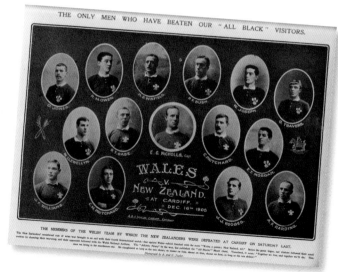

Above: A momentous day in Welsh rugby was 16th December, 1905, when Wales beat the visiting All-Blacks at Cardiff Arms Park.

Above left: A newspaper report details the defeat of the Welsh team by Scotland 11–8 on 3rd February, 1923, at Cardiff Arms Park.

Left: Collectors' item: this complimentary ticket allowed the lucky bearer to witness Wales defeat France 8–3 on 23rd February, 1929.

Remarkably, though, the new National Stadium was only to be a short-lived home of Welsh rugby. Within little more than a decade it had been decided that it wasn't big enough and its facilities were inadequate. It was demolished and replaced by the Millennium Stadium, which opened in June 1999. The Millennium Stadium is on roughly a North-South axis, whereas the previous National Stadium was roughly East-West. In an act of pragmatism forced by lack of funding, the North Stand of the Millennium Stadium and the South Stand of the Cardiff RFC ground are actually the same structure.

During the early 2000s the Millennium Stadium was used by the Football Association as a base for the English FA and League Cup Finals while the new Wembley Stadium was being built.

The Cardiff RFC ground still exists and still bears the name 'Cardiff Arms Park'. In 2009 the Cardiff Blues Rugby team moved away from the Arms Park to share a new stadium, the Cardiff City Stadium, on the outskirts of the city, with Cardiff City Football Club. However, they have returned to the Arms Park for the occasional match. A semi-professional team, Cardiff RFC, still play at the Arms Park and, despite some concern about the future ownership of the ground, remain confident that they will continue to play rugby there for many years to come.

In a fitting link with the past, the choral tradition of Welsh rugby has passed on to the Millennium Stadium and *Land of My Fathers* is still regularly and rousingly belted out at the 21st-century home of the Welsh National team.

ISLAND FARM
PRISONER OF WAR CAMP

51° 29' 40" N, 3° 34' 55" W

11TH MARCH, 1945

ISLAND FARM ROAD, BRIDGEND, MID-GLAMORGAN, CF31 3LY

Above: Hut 9 is the only part of the former Island Farm PoW camp that remains. The basic structure has been granted listed buildings status.

SCENE OF A GREAT PoW ESCAPE

British accounts of the Second World War are full of tales of daring-do by Allied prisoners of war in German camps, including escapes from such strongholds as Colditz. Less well-known is the experience of German and Italian PoWs held in Britain at the hundreds of camps dotted all over the country, including their escape attempts.

On Sunday 11th March, 1945 what may well have been the largest mass breakout from a prisoner of war camp during the Second World War took place not on German soil but in Britain – at the Island Farm Camp near Bridgend in South Wales. In the true tradition of escape tunnels, the German prisoners prepared their bid for freedom over a long period, tunnelling under cover of communal singing to disguise the noise. They used a variety of implements to dig the tunnel and found ingenious ways of disposing of the spoil. They even built a false wall in one of the huts and dropped balls of excavated clay through a hole into the cavity to conceal the spoil from their excavation works.

TUNNEL BREAKOUT

At about 10pm that night they escaped. Most were recaptured in the local area, although some are reported to have reached as far as Birmingham and Southampton. At the time the official figure was put at 70 escapees, but it has been claimed that as many as 86 may have escaped and that some may have evaded

Above: Built to house workers at a nearby munitions factory, the escalation of the war saw Island Farm drafted into service as a PoW camp.

significant increase in PoWs, so extra accommodation was needed, and Island Farm was pressed into service. The camp initially housed a mixture of German and Italian detainees but, by November 1944, it had become a camp for German officers only.

After the breakout in March 1945, all Island Farm's prisoners were transferred elsewhere and the camp was later used to house very senior German officers – many of whom were awaiting war crimes trials after the end of the war. The camp finally closed in 1948. One of the accommodation units, Hut 9, remains standing and has been designated as a listed building.

SPORTING CHANCE

capture and returned home to Germany. If that were true, the Island Farm escape should be regarded as the most successful PoW escape of the war. Only 76 escaped from Stalag Luft 3 in Germany – a feat that was the inspiration for the film *The Great Escape*.

Island Farm had only become a prisoner of war camp towards the end of the war. It had originally been built as a hostel for workers at a nearby munitions factory and was later used as a barracks for Americans preparing for the Allied invasion of France. However, after the D-Day landings in June 1944, there was a

For more than a half a century since, a variety of schemes have come and gone for the use of the site, including the idea of creating a national rugby stadium for Wales there before the site of Cardiff Arms Park was eventually redeveloped. However, in June 2011 the local council approved plans for a major sports complex on the site. The complex would include stadia for rugby union, rugby league and football as well as tennis courts and a swimming pool. The remaining PoW camp hut would be retained in the development.

Left: Outline plans for the redevelopment of the site as Island Farm Sports Village, by local developer HD Limited, include the construction of a 15,000-seater stadium for Rugby League and Rugby Union, a 5,000-seater stadium for Bridgend Ravens RFC, a sports centre, a swimming pool, two sports halls and squash courts, a tennis centre, a boxing centre and a 2,000-seater football stand, plus more than 40 acres of land devoted to nature conservation.

TONYPANDY
RIOT SCENE

51° 37' 31" N, 3° 27' 26" W

8TH NOVEMBER, 1910

LLWYNYPIA ROAD, TONYPANDY, MID-GLAMORGAN, CF40 2EW

A DEFINING MOMENT THAT SULLIED CHURCHILL'S REPUTATION

Above: In a comparatively peaceful demonstration, a large crowd gathered at the mouth of the pit on 12th November, 1910, four days after the pitched battles with police in the centre of Tonypandy.

Left: Home Secretary, Winston Churchill, on 1st November, 1910, the week before the events at Tonypandy. Dispute prevails over his exact role in sending troops and police reinforcements to control the rioting miners.

The area known as Tonypandy Square, near The Pandy public house, is an unremarkable spot. However, it occupies an important place in the history and folklore of trade unionism and the wider Labour movement. The events of November 1910 in Tonypandy in the Rhondda Valley still have a special significance more than a century later. They were a defining moment in the battle between capital and labour and helped to define positions that influenced events for many years. In addition, the role played

by Winston Churchill, then the Home Secretary, was controversial and meant that his reputation in South Wales remained sullied even after he became Britain's wartime hero many years later.

The events that became known as the 'Tonypandy Riots' took place in several locations in the Rhondda over a number of days. However, the main disturbance took place on the night of Tuesday, 8th November, 1910 when striking miners and police fought each other and strikers attacked shops and businesses in the centre of the town.

The disturbances were the culmination of a dispute that had begun two months earlier when mine owners locked out nearly a thousand miners from the nearby Ely colliery in a pay dispute. The miners reacted by going on strike. The owners brought in workers from elsewhere to break the strike, but by the beginning of November, picketing by the striking miners had closed every pit in the area apart from the Glamorgan Colliery at Llwynypia.

PICKET LINES

On Sunday, 6th November, striking miners picketed Llwynypia in an attempt to stop strike breakers entering the colliery. Some of the pickets started stoning the building and there were struggles between miners and the police guarding the colliery. The clashes became more violent and the strikers were pushed back by repeated baton charges by police. A demonstration in the town centre was broken up by police and a number of properties were damaged and there was some looting.

The local Chief Constable called for reinforcements from the War Office. There is some dispute about Winston Churchill's exact role in the events. It appears he despatched police reinforcements and troops, although he also appears to have advised against the deployment of the troops unless absolutely necessary. Nevertheless, a detachment of the 18th Hussars was

deployed in the area the following day, when extensive clashes took place. Nearly 600 people, including 80 police, were injured.

There was one confirmed death – apparently the result of being hit by a police baton. There were plenty of rumours that police fired shots, but there is no conclusive evidence of that. When 13 striking miners appeared in court the following month, there were mass demonstrations of up to 10,000 people in support of them.

The dispute ended the following year. Glamorgan Colliery closed in 1945. In a way, though, the most persistent legacy of the Tonypandy Riots was the impact on Churchill's reputation. Whatever the true facts about the deployment of troops and their behaviour, the accepted view in the area was that Churchill had sent in troops to shoot at strikers. The repercussions were felt for many years. During the Second World War, there were suggestions that the Labour Party might not support Churchill in the wartime coalition because of the legacy of Tonypandy. Even after Churchill's death, the ill-feeling persisted. In 2010, a hundred years after the event, a local council in Wales objected to the idea of renaming a military base in the area after Churchill.

Today, the layout of the centre of Tonypandy is much the same as it was in 1910 and many of the buildings attacked during the disturbances are still there. The centenary of the riots were extensively marked in Tonypandy in 2010.

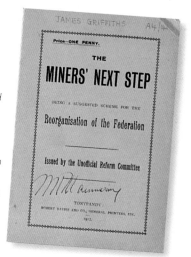

Left: Robert Thomas's monumental bronze sculpture, depicting a miner and his family, was erected by the Rhondda Civic Society in October 1993 to commemorate the mining communities of the area. It is located on the A4119 near Llwynypia, which figured prominently in the riots.

Right: The Miners' Next Step was an economic and political pamphlet, produced in 1912, calling for miners to embrace syndicalism and a new trade unionism. The pamphlet was written by Noah Ablett of the Unofficial Reform Committee.

SENGHENYDD MINING
DISASTER

51° 36′ 28″ N, 3° 16′ 37″ W

14TH OCTOBER, 1913   COMMERCIAL STREET, SENGHENYDD, CAERPHILLY, GWENT, CF83 4GY

BRITAIN'S WORST MINING TRAGEDY

Almost a thousand men and boys were below ground at the Universal Colliery at Senghenydd near Caerphilly, on the morning of Tuesday, 14th October, 1913. This was a highly profitable era for the Welsh mining industry with demand for coal boosted by the military build-up prior to the First World War. Much of the product of the Universal Colliery and other pits was used to fuel the battleships of the Royal Navy.

At around 8am an enormous explosion ripped through the pit. The cause of the explosion was never definitively established but it's thought it was almost certainly the result of an electrical spark igniting 'firedamp' or methane. The spark probably came from an electric bell. The initial explosion raised coal dust, which then ignited causing a chain reaction through the pit. Many miners were killed by fire or the explosion but others would have been asphyxiated by a lethal combination of noxious gases.

A total of 440 men and boys were killed in the

explosion despite the heroic efforts of rescue teams brought in from neighbouring areas. The rescue operation was hampered by the strength of the fires underground, the debris caused by the explosions and roof falls. People were pulled from the wreckage days after the explosion. However, the loss of life at Senghenydd makes this the worst mining disaster in British history and one of the worst colliery accidents internationally.

GUILTY PARTIES

Following the disaster, an inquiry concluded that the mine owners and managers were at fault but prosecutions that followed resulted in fines of only £24 against the mine manager and £10 against the owners. This was all the more remarkable because the events of 1913 were the second major tragedy to befall the pit in little more than a decade. In 1901, 81 people had died after an explosion at Universal and a series of recommendations had been made for improving safety then.

After the 1913 tragedy, work at the mine was resumed just over a month later and full production was achieved by 1916. However, Universal's life was to be short-lived and the pit lasted only until 1928, when production ceased. Universal Colliery later became a ventilation tunnel for another neighbouring pit but it was eventually filled in 1979.

There are no visible remains of the pit in Senghenydd today. Nant-y-parc Primary School stands on the site of the mine. There is a memorial to those who died in the school grounds and an annual service of remembrance is held there. In 2012 plans were underway for the building of a more substantial memorial in the town in time for the centenary of the disaster in 2013.

Although Britain's worst mining tragedy took place a hundred years ago, more recent mining tragedies, also in South Wales, have shown that, even in the much smaller mining industry of the 21st century, the dangers of working underground have not been eliminated.

Facing page: Rescue operations at the Universal Colliery in Senghenydd, after the explosion that wrecked the pit head gear and set half the 'Lancaster' pit ablaze, with a loss of some 440 men and boys, who were trapped underground at the time.

Above: The families of the trapped miners wait anxiously for news of their loved ones, entombed in the stricken pit.

Above: The bodies of the dead miners were brought to the surface, days after the explosion, by the team of rescue workers.

Above: A memorial at the site of the former Universal Colliery, erected in 1981, commemorates the men who died in the 1901 and 1913 accidents.

THE TRAGEDY OF
ABERFAN

51° 44' 55" N, 3° 22' 53" W

21st OCTOBER, 1966

MOY ROAD, ABERFAN, MID GLAMORGAN, CF48 4QR

Above: The scene at Aberfan, Glamorgan, after the man-made mountain of pit waste slid down onto Pantglas School and a row of houses, killing 116 children and 28 adults.

144 DEAD AS A TORRENT OF MINING RUBBLE
ENGULFS A PRIMARY SCHOOL

It was the last day before half-term. On the morning of Friday, 21st October, 1966, the children of the Pantglas Junior School in the village of Aberfan near Merthyr Tydfil, Wales, were singing *All Things Bright and Beautiful* in morning assembly. Unbeknown to them and their teachers, about 5,300 cubic feet of debris, saturated by recent rainfall, had broken loose from the colliery waste-tip high above the village and was heading at great speed down the hillside. At around 9.15 that morning a 40 feet deep landslide of mining waste crashed into the western edge of the village engulfing a farm, 20 houses and burying the primary school.

There were frantic rescue efforts once the landslide

Above: the avalanche of coal sludge that engulfed part of the mining village of Aberfan reveals the full scope of the tragic event.

Above: The path of the rain-soaked slurry is clearly shown in this aerial photograph of Aberfan as teams of rescue workers battle to find survivors.

had stopped, with parents and others tearing at the rubble with their bare hands. However, the torrent had done its damage within a matter of seconds. A few survivors were pulled from the scene but the final death toll was 144, including 116 children – almost half the population of the school. More than 2,000 people attended the joint funeral for most of the victims held the following Thursday at the nearby Bryntaf Cemetery.

Aberfan was one of the first major disasters of the television age. Live outside broadcast vehicles were despatched and the tragedy touched millions, who contributed to a disaster fund that had reached over £1.6m (about £25m at 2012 values) within a few months. The disaster provoked national and international sympathy but also widespread anger, particularly in the mining communities of South Wales.

UNHEEDED WARNINGS

The anger was focused on the National Coal Board (NCB) and its Chairman Lord Robens. On the day of the disaster he was due to be installed as the Chancellor of the University of Surrey and, rather than heading for South Wales, he decided to go ahead with the university ceremony, only arriving in Aberfan the following day. At first he maintained that the NCB was blameless, describing the tragedy as a natural accident caused by "unknown springs" below the colliery tip.

However, the public inquiry established under Lord Justice Edmund Davies, which sat for 76 days and reported in August 1967, concluded that the disaster was entirely the fault of the NCB. It had failed to have any policy in place for waste tipping from its mines. Worse still, the inquiry concluded that the NCB had known about the instability of the colliery tip above Aberfan, but neither local officials nor the senior management of the NCB had heeded the warnings. In a particularly damming section of his report, Lord Edmund Davies concluded that Aberfan was "a terrifying tale of bungling ineptitude... of failure to heed clear warnings... and of decent men led astray by foolishness or ignorance".

Legislation was subsequently enacted to tighten up the control of colliery tips. The NCB was ordered to pay compensation to the victims' families – of £500 per child – but no NCB officials were disciplined or sacked and none faced any criminal prosecutions. Lord Robens, who had made a dramatic admission of NCB

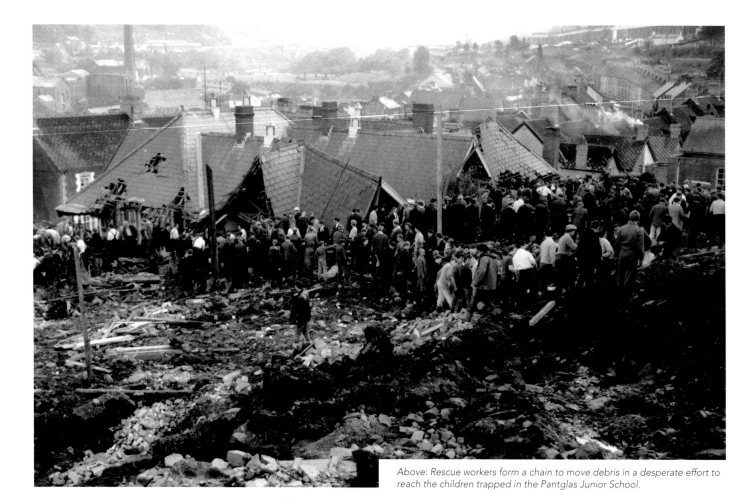

Above: Rescue workers form a chain to move debris in a desperate effort to reach the children trapped in the Pantglas Junior School.

liability at the concluding stages of the inquiry, then offered to resign when the report was published, but his offer of resignation was refused. At the inquest into the children's deaths, some parents vented their anger against the NCB describing them as "murderers".

There was a further controversy over the NCB's refusal to pay the full cost of the removal of other slag heaps around Aberfan. The Aberfan Disaster Fund had to contribute £150,000 towards the cost of having them removed. It wasn't until 1997 that the incoming Labour Government paid back £150,000 into the fund to cover this cost, although there was disquiet in Aberfan that the grant did not allow for the considerable inflation in the intervening period. However, in 2007, the devolved Welsh Government made a £2m donation to the fund.

The psychological impact of the events of 21st October, 1966 continues. A study published in 2003 found that more than half the survivors of the disaster had suffered post-traumatic stress disorder at some time in their lives and more than a third still suffered from sleeping problems and experienced bad dreams related to the disaster.

Merthyr Tydfil Colliery closed in 1989. Pantglas Junior School was demolished and a memorial garden stands on the site of where the school was engulfed. There is also a memorial in Bryntaf Cemetery where many of the victims are buried.

Many of the families affected by the tragedy still live in Aberfan and the disaster is still very much part of the life of the community. Considerable numbers of tourists, including school parties learning about Aberfan as part of Welsh history, visit the memorials on what is now a peaceful side street on the edge of a sleepy village in the Welsh valleys.

Above: The roof of the Pantglas Junior School stands above the mound of pit slurry that engulfed the building.

Above: Teams of soldiers and miners work only with shovels amid the wreckage in Aberfan.

Above: The graves of many of the children who died in the Aberfan disaster are located in the Bryntaf Cemetery, a section of the Aberfan Cemetery opened in 1915. The rows of headstones act as a poignant reminder of the scale of the tragedy.

GLOUCESTER HOUSE OF
HORRORS

51° 51' 42" N, 2° 14' 36" W

1972–1994

25 CROMWELL STREET, GLOUCESTER, GL1 1RE

THE HOUSE WHERE INFAMOUS ATROCITIES WERE COMMITTED

Some events, some crimes in particular, are so unspeakable that the locations associated with them can never escape the association. Number 25 Cromwell Street in Gloucester was one such place. It was there that Fred and Rose West raped and murdered young girls, including their own children.

The Wests are known to have murdered at least 11 girls and women between 1971 and 1987, including three members of their own families. Their other victims were mainly lodgers, who they had lured there. It's a desperately sad tale of incest, prostitution, rape and murder – most of it happening in an anonymous residential street not far from the centre of the historic city of Gloucester. Most of their victims were buried in the garden. Both the Wests had troubled childhoods and both apparently came from families where incest was the norm.

They were eventually caught when one of their daughters spoke at school about being raped and police launched an investigation. Fred West was charged in July 1994 but he committed suicide in January 1995, while in prison on remand. Rose West was tried in 1995 and given life for 10 murders.

Some famous crime addresses remain – for example, the homes in North London where Dennis Nilsen murdered young men, cut them up and disposed of them in the drains. Others are no more. The house in Soham in Cambridgeshire where Ian Huntley murdered Holly Wells and Jessica Chapman in 2003 was demolished after his conviction. Years earlier 10 Rillington Place in West London, where John Christie murdered at least eight women, was also knocked down and the whole street renamed.

MEMORIES ERASED

In Gloucester they went to extraordinary lengths to obliterate the memory of the Wests' crimes and to prevent ghoulish trophy hunters. The City Council bought the house and the adjoining number 23 and, in October 1996, demolition took place. A concrete cap was placed over the plot. All the debris from the demolition and the fittings from the house were crushed and disposed of at a council tip.

A public consultation exercise was undertaken after the demolition to help decide what should be done with the site. The area where the house once stood is now a simple walkway linking Cromwell Street and St Michael's Square. Plans for a memorial garden were rejected as this was thought likely to encourage sightseers.

However, the fate of the wrought-iron address sign '25 Cromwell Street', which came to symbolise the murders, remains a matter of dispute more than 15 years on. There was a legal row over its ownership and in 2012 it remained in the custody of Gloucestershire Police.

Facing page: A policeman stands guard outside 25 Cromwell Street, Gloucester, its windows blocked up. Demolition was due to start on the former home of Fred and Rosemary West in October 1996. Inset: an undated sinister snapshot of mass murderers Fred and Rosemary West.

Above right: Demolition underway on 25 Cromwell Street and the adjoining house, to eradicate all traces of the notorious address where victims of the Wests were killed and buried.

Right: The area where the Wests' house stood has become a simple walkway linking Cromwell Street with St Michael's Square.

IFFLEY ROAD
RUNNING
TRACK

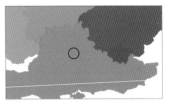

51° 44' 53" N, 1° 14' 36" W

6TH MAY, 1954   ROGER BANNISTER RUNNING TRACK, IFFLEY ROAD SPORTS COMPLEX, OXFORD, OX4 1EQ

THE FIRST TIME ANYONE HAD RUN A MILE IN UNDER FOUR MINUTES

Above: Medical student Roger Bannister hits the tape at an athletics meeting in Oxford and the world's first sub-four minute mile has been run – in three minutes, fifty-nine-point-four seconds.

In a way Iffley Road Running Track in Oxford hasn't changed in more than 50 years. Students who dream of running fast and breaking world records still come to this ground to train and to compete as they did in the 1950s. The film of Roger Bannister running a sub-four minute mile in 1954 shows a black-and-white world of wooden grandstands, cinder tracks and spectators in long gaberdine raincoats. Nowadays, the scene appears more vibrant, with a colourful synthetic track and the concrete that characterises sports grounds in an era where safety has a higher priority. But the objective remains the same.

What happened on Thursday, 6th May, 1954 was the culmination of many years of rivalry and planning. Running a mile in under four minutes was, like covering the 100 metres in under 10 seconds, one of the holy grails of athletics. Before the Second World War, another English athlete, Sydney Wooderson, had established a record for the mile, at a race in London in 1937, of 4 minutes 6.4 seconds. Two Swedes, Arne Andersson and Gunder Hägg, brought the record down during the war years and it stood at 4 minutes 1.4 seconds in 1945.

ATHLETIC GOAL

Bannister started running when he was a student at Oxford in the late 1940s. He was inspired by Wooderson and by watching the 1948 London Olympics. He competed in the 1952 Olympics in Helsinki but was disappointed to finish fourth in the 1500 metres and considered giving up running. Instead, he set himself the goal of being the first to run a sub-four minute mile.

During 1953 Bannister intensified his attempts but others were also trying to get there, notably the Australian, John Landy, who got within two seconds of the target in late 1953 and early 1954. With the Australian season over in April 1954, Bannister knew he had an opportunity to beat Landy to the record if he acted quickly.

The record attempt was made at a scheduled meeting between the British Amateur Athletics Association and Bannister's old university. The event was widely anticipated. BBC Radio covered the race live and more than 3,000 spectators were there to watch it. Bannister nearly called off the attempt because of strong winds earlier in the day but the wind dropped and the attempt went ahead.

Above: Sir Roger Bannister with his old running shoes on the 50th anniversary of the first sub-four-minute mile, at Pembroke College, Oxford, on 6th May, 2004.

VITAL SECONDS

Chris Brasher and Christopher Chattaway acted as his pacemakers. The first lap was completed in 57.5 seconds; the half-mile in 1 minute 58 seconds; the third lap in 3 minutes 0.7 seconds. In Bannister's own account of the race, he talks about the final section of the race: "There being no pain, only a great unity of movement and aim. I felt at that moment it was my one chance to do one thing supremely well". The race commentator, Norris MacWhirter, announced the result and Bannister's exact time – 3 minutes 59.4 seconds – but his announcement was drowned out by the cheering crowds.

Bannister's record stood for little over a month until it was beaten by John Landy at a meeting in Finland. In August 1954 the men competed at the Commonwealth Games in Vancouver with Bannister victorious. Roger Bannister retired from running and went on to a successful career in medicine as a neurologist. He was also the first Chairman of the Sports Council.

The Iffley Road track is now part of the Oxford University Sports Complex. In 2007, in honour of what happened on 6th May, 1954, another great British middle distance runner, Sebastian Coe, named the track 'The Roger Bannister Running Track' at a ceremony attended by Bannister. In 2012 floodlights were installed but the track that Olympic hopefuls run on in the 21st century still follows the same course as Bannister did when he made history more than half a century ago.

ALEXANDRA PALACE
TV STATION

51° 35' 40" N, -0° 7' 48" E

2ND NOVEMBER, 1936   ALEXANDRA PALACE, ALEXANDRA PALACE WAY, LONDON, N22 7AY

Above: Girls from London's Windmill Theatre perform at a dress rehearsal for a televised programme at Alexandra Palace, on 4th April, 1946.

Above: Ready for their close-up. The Windmill girls pose for a group head shot in front of the television camera.

THE START OF A REGULAR PUBLIC TELEVISION SERVICE IN BRITAIN

Like most new technologies, the story of the birth of television is a long and complicated one. However, 2nd November, 1936, at Alexandra Palace in North London, can rightly be regarded as the day and the place when television broadcasting began in a meaningful sense.

It was a typically British way of doing things. What began on that autumn day was actually a public trial of two rival systems – the EMI all electrical system and the Baird, partly mechanical, system. From the 1920s and into the 1930s a number of scientists and engineers, with John Logie Baird prominent among them, had been working on trials of television. However, in 1935 the British Government decided that television should be taken seriously and set up a television advisory committee, chaired by Lord Selsdon, to recommend what should happen. The committee was unable to decide which system should be used, so they decided that two leading television companies would go head to head in a public trial over a six-month period.

Above: The ballet Les Sylphides, performed by Ballet Rambert in front of television cameras at Alexandra Palace, on 22nd October, 1949. Annette Chapell, leading dancer of the troupe, takes centre stage.

Above: The Palm Court Entrance of Alexandra Palace, which was hosting the World Darts Championship, on 19th December, 2007.

Alexandra Palace was a pragmatic choice for the studios for this groundbreaking service. Its main advantage was its height above sea level. Once a TV mast had been constructed, the top was 600 feet above sea level, which enabled the signal to radiate 30 miles. Alexandra Palace had been opened in 1873 as a place of education, entertainment and recreation. It was envisaged as the 'People's Palace' and was seen as a North London rival to Crystal Palace in South London. In 1935, the BBC took a lease on part of the building and began converting rooms into the necessary facilities for the TV trial. Two studios were built – Studio A for Marconi-EMI and Studio B for Baird Television Limited.

On the opening night, by the toss of a coin, the Baird system broadcast first. The opening transmission consisted of a formal opening ceremony, a Movietone newsreel and a variety show. The EMI system then broadcast the exact same programme afterwards. It is estimated that no more than about 400 homes had television sets, which cost the equivalent of a small car at the time.

The service that began in 1936 is now often referred to as the world's first regular high-definition television service. This is not to be confused with the high-definition TV we talk about in the 21st century. In 1936 high-definition meant television of at least 240 lines compared with earlier TV experiments that had been as low as 30 lines.

RIVAL BROADCASTERS

The rival systems broadcast on alternate weeks, but it soon became clear that the Marconi-EMI system was superior. It was more flexible and less cumbersome. The EMI cameras were moveable. Baird's intermediate film cameras were fixed and employed a complicated and potentially dangerous method of shooting film and processing it immediately in a water solution involving cyanide. The six month trial never ran its course. It was decided to go with the EMI system and the Baird studio closed on 30th January, 1937.

The BBC TV service continued at 'Ally Pally' until 1939, but was shut down when war broke out. After the war, the television staff returned and BBC TV resumed on 7th June, 1946. The following day saw the first post-war outside broadcast of the Victory Parade to celebrate the end of the Second World War. Alexandra Palace continued to play a pivotal role in the development of television for more than 30 years. Programmes were made there until 1954, but they then transferred to Lime Grove in West London and subsequently to the new Television Centre. However, Ally Pally remained the main base of BBC TV News until 1969. From 1970 until 1981, the studios were used for Open University broadcasts.

As well as its crucial role in the history of television, Alexandra Palace itself has a fascinating history. The 1873 palace was destroyed by a fire 16 days after it opened. It was quickly rebuilt and reopened in 1875. It had its own railway line and station and there was a racecourse in the grounds until 1970. In July 1981 another major fire severely damaged more than half

Above: An aerial photograph of Alexandra Palace, in March 2004. The Palace itself covers seven acres and is surrounded by 196 acres of parkland, and grounds that include a pub and restaurant, an ice rink, a boating lake, a pitch-and-putt course, 1,500 free parking spaces.

of the building. The future of Alexandra Palace itself has been the subject of controversy since then. Local residents were bitterly opposed to plans by Haringey Council to turn the building over to mainly commercial use. It remains run by a charitable trust and survives into the 21st century as a live music, sports and events venue.

The original Ally Pally studios still exist and are jealously guarded by a group of TV historians and enthusiasts. In 2011, on the 75th anniversary of the first broadcast, special celebrations were held at the Palace. Attempts to designate the studios a UNESCO World Heritage site have been underway since 2011.

A public consultation was held in 2012 about plans to upgrade the Palace, including opening up the BBC studios to visitors.

Exactly four weeks after the world's first public television service opened at Alexandra Palace in North London, the Crystal Palace in South London burned to the ground. These two events in the same month of November 1936 somehow together symbolise the passing of one era of entertainment and the start of another. It is not an exaggeration to say that what happened on a North London hilltop in 1936 marked the proper arrival of the most influential medium of the 20th century.

HIGHBURY
STADIUM
REDEVELOPMENT

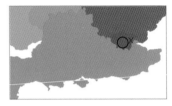

51° 33' 34" N, -0° 6' 11" E

1913–2006

HIGHBURY SQUARE, AVENALL ROAD, HIGHBURY, LONDON N5 1DP

Above: The East Stand of Highbury, home of Arsenal FC, on 15th August, 1950.

Above: The shells of the art deco East and West stands were retained as an integral part of the apartment development.

Above: The East Stand on Avenell Road shortly before redevelopment into flats.

FORMER HOME OF ARSENAL FC NOW
LUXURY FLATS

Since the 1990s three factors have conspired to make many football clubs move to new grounds – more stringent safety requirements, the opportunity to make more money by increasing capacity and the vanity of owners and chairmen. Of the grounds that have disappeared as a result, Highbury Stadium, the former home of Arsenal FC in North London, has one of the most glamorous histories.

Highbury, or Arsenal Stadium to give it its correct title, was built, as were many football grounds at the time, by the great stadium architect, Archibald Leitch. It opened in 1913 when Arsenal, originally Woolwich Arsenal, had moved from South to North London. In the 1930s, Highbury acquired its distinctive art deco

East and West stands and it was further redeveloped in the 1980s and 1990s, when the ends behind both goals became all-seater.

For nearly a hundred years, Highbury was the home of the one of the most consistently successful club sides in the country. Arsenal enjoyed several periods of great success: in the 1930s, under manager Herbert Chapman, with players such as Cliff Bastin and Alex James; in the late 1960s and early 1970s; and more recently, under their long-serving French manager, Arsène Wenger. Highbury witnessed many great games and a number of England internationals were played there. In 1966 Highbury was the venue for the world heavyweight boxing bout between Henry Cooper and Muhammad Ali.

However, in 2006, Arsenal played their last match at the stadium, having decided that its capacity of just under 40,000 was insufficient in the big money era of the Premier League. Thierry Henry scored the last competitive goal at Highbury on 7th May against Wigan Athletic. Arsenal moved to a new stadium, the Emirates, just a few hundred yards from Highbury.

Highbury was redeveloped into a complex of luxury apartments and affordable homes. The listed façades of the two art deco stands from the 1930s were retained and the pitch was redeveloped into a communal garden for the 711 flats that now exist in four blocks, where the four stands once stood. There is also a car park under the pitch, and a gym. If ever there was a redevelopment that was sympathetic to a site's history, then this is it.

Above: A Premier League match in progress between Arsenal and Coventry City, on 11th August, 1997, which The Gunners won 2–0, with goals by Ian Wright.

Above right: The Highbury Square development utilised the East and West stands and added luxury accommodation where the other two stands once stood. The pitch became elegant communal gardens.

Right: The clean lines of the classic art deco façade of the East Stand survive in the Highbury Square redevelopment, maintaining the building's link to its footballing history.

RADIO CAROLINE
BEACHED

51° 49' 51" N, 1° 14' 54 " E

OFF THE COAST OF FRINTON-ON-SEA, ESSEX, CO13 9AT

THE PIRATES OFF THE ESSEX COAST WHO CHANGED THE FACE OF BRITISH RADIO

Above: On 20th January, 1966, the MV Mi Amigo, from which the pirate station Radio Caroline broacast, lost its anchor in a storm and ran aground on the beach at Frinton-on-Sea. The crew and broadcasting staff were rescued unharmed by breeches buoy, but the ship's hull was damaged and repairs had to be carried out at Zaandam, Netherlands.

With hundreds of UK-based radio stations operating legally and thousands available via the web in the 21st century, it's difficult to believe that in 1966 there were only three legal radio stations in Britain. The Home Service (now Radio 4), the Light Programme (now Radio 2) and the Third Programme (now Radio 3) were all run by the BBC. However, the development of rock and roll, and pop music in general, in the 1950s and 1960s meant there was a demand for radio to cater for this interest – an interest to which the BBC had largely failed to respond.

The vacuum was filled by pirate radio. This was radio broadcasting from ships anchored just outside British territorial waters to avoid the legal sanctions they would have faced had they broadcast onshore. Radio Caroline was the most famous of these. It began broadcasting from MV *Caroline* off Felixstowe in Suffolk in March 1964. Meanwhile, a rival, Radio Atlanta, started broadcasting from MV *Mi Amigo* off Frinton-on-sea on the Essex coast in April of the same year. In July of 1964 the two stations merged. The *Caroline* moved to a mooring off the Isle of Man to target the North of England, while the *Mi Amigo* remained off the Essex coast aiming its broadcasts at London and the South East.

Radio Caroline's main rival was Radio London (otherwise known as the Big L), which was also moored off Frinton-on-sea. This genteel Essex resort was thus home to the two most significant pirate stations that were to change the face of radio forever. Both stations attracted huge audiences estimated at running into tens of millions. Many of the DJs who broadcast from them became household names, including Tony Blackburn, Simon Dee and Dave Lee Travis.

ALL AT SEA

The lives of these pirate stations were not without incident. Perhaps the most famous was on 20th January, 1966 when the *Mi Amigo* broke free from its moorings in a storm and ran aground on the beach between Frinton and Walton. The crew and DJs were all rescued unharmed but the ship was seriously damaged, and had to be towed to the Netherlands for repairs. While the *Mi Amigo* was undergoing repairs, Radio Caroline kept broadcasting from an alternative ship borrowed from a Swedish pirate station. It wasn't until late April that the *Mi Amigo* was able to return to the waters off Frinton and resume normal service.

A year later, 1967 marked the turning point for pirate radio. The British Government brought in the Marine Offences Act, which effectively closed most pirates down and, in September of that year, the BBC started Radio One broadcasting pop music. Many of the operators of pirate radio became legal broadcasters and some of the entrepreneurs who were behind the stations subsequently got involved in legal commercial radio when it started in Britain in the early 1970s.

The breeches buoys used in the rescue of Radio Caroline in 1966 are preserved in the local museum

at Walton. Radio Caroline continued broadcasting in various guises and continues into the 21st century as a mainly internet-based station. The MV *Mi Amigo*, however, sank off the Kent coast in a storm in 1980. For a further six years the mast remained visible but it broke up in 1986 and a ship that had played such a key part in the development of radio was no more.

Left: A Home Office photograph of a tape cover revealing the playlist of Radio Caroline DJ Phillip Marshall (alias 'Mitchell'), from 4th September, 1975.

Left: The 45RPM single Ev'rybody's Gonna Be Happy by the Kinks, in a sleeve promoting Radio Caroline.

Above: L–R, Radio Caroline DJs Paul Noble, John Sydner, Keith Skues, Colin Nicol and Brian Vaughan aboard the Mi Amigo on 11th August, 1965.

Above: Johnnie Walker began broadcasting for pirate station Swinging Radio England before moving to Radio Caroline.

Above: Dave Lee Travis joined Radio Caroline in 1965 and moved to BBC Radio 1 in 1968 where he remained until 1993.

Above: Tony Blackburn, who worked on Radio Caroline in the 1960s, was the first DJ to broadcast on BBC Radio 1 in 1967.

Above: Simon Dee, seen here with The Beatles, joined Radio Caroline in 1964, and later became a TV chat show host.

OLD CAVENDISH
LABORATORIES
CAMBRIDGE

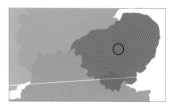

52° 12' 11" N, 0° 7' 7" E

28TH FEBRUARY, 1953   NEW MUSEUMS SITE, FREE SCHOOL LANE, CAMBRIDGE, CB2 3QH

THE MOST IMPORTANT PLACE OF SCIENTIFIC DISCOVERY IN THE WORLD?

Above: American molecular biologist, geneticist and zoologist, James D. Watson, co-discoverer of the structure of DNA, pictured in 2012.

Above: Watson's joint Nobel Prizewinner, English molecular biologist, biophysicist and neuroscientist, Francis Crick, pictured in 2004.

Although this location in the centre of Cambridge feels very much part of the academic tradition of the city, it does not conjure up a feeling of cutting edge scientific research. Nevertheless, it was here, in Free School Lane, a fairly unprepossessing street, that the 'secret of life' was discovered.

It was in February 1953 that the British physicist Francis Crick and the American James Watson discovered the double helix structure of DNA. As with many discoveries and inventions, there remains some controversy over whether they deserve all the credit, or whether some of it should be shared with others. However, it is widely accepted that it was their crucial contribution that led

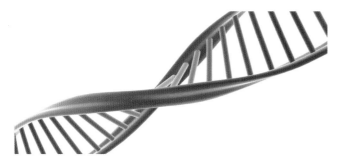

Above: The double helix structure of DNA, a nucleic acid containing the genetic instructions used in the development and functioning of all known living organisms, discovered by Crick and Watson.

to an understanding of the role of DNA. They were awarded a Nobel Prize for their work. After they had made their discovery, it is said they went to the nearby Eagle pub to celebrate and Crick remarked "We have discovered the secret of life".

SCIENTIFIC FIRSTS

The contribution of the Old Cavendish Laboratories to the history of scientific discovery doesn't end there. Earlier, it had been the scene of several other major breakthroughs. In 1932, John Cockroft and Ernest Walton carried out what is generally known as the first splitting of the atom.

The Old Cavendish Laboratories had originally been built from the 1870s onwards on the site where the University's Botanic Gardens had previously stood. At the time the labs were seen as cutting edge, but were deliberately built in a traditional style to fit in with the ambience of the surroundings and to reassure traditionalists within the university that their building did not represent a move away from established methods of teaching.

In 1975, the Cavendish Laboratories had outgrown the site and they relocated to West Cambridge. The buildings where some of the most important scientific discoveries of the 20th century were made are still in use by Cambridge University as lecture halls and examination rooms.

Watson and Crick's achievements are marked by a plaque near the site of the Old Cavendish Labs and another at The Eagle public house. There is also a golden helix over the door of the house in Portugal Place in Cambridge where Crick used to live.

Above: The Old Cavendish Laboratories in Free School Lane, Cambridge, which have witnessed numerous scientific discoveries. Below: The Laboratory of Physical Chemistry, where Joseph John Thomson discovered the electron in 1897.

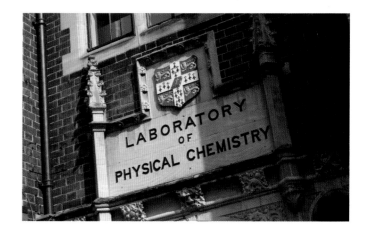

KEGWORTH PLANE
CRASH

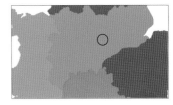

52° 50' 21" N, 1° 17' 45" W

8TH JANUARY, 1989

M1 MOTORWAY NEAR KEGWORTH, LEICESTERSHIRE, DE74 2DA

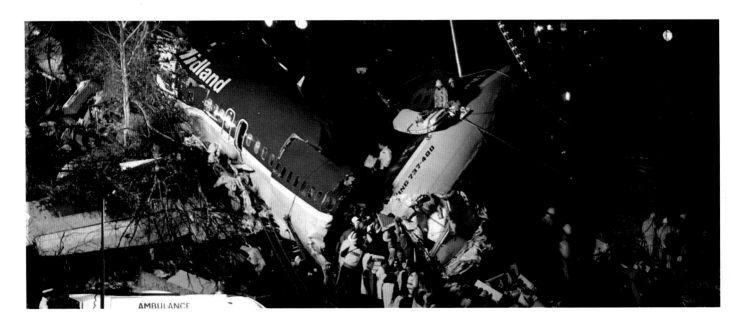

AMBULANCE

PLANE CRASHES ONTO A MOTORWAY

It might have been imagined as a scene from an action movie – a plane crashing onto a motorway. But on Sunday, 8th January, 1989 it happened for real when a British Midland Airways flight, en route from London to Belfast, came down on the M1 motorway just short of the runway, while attempting an emergency landing at East Midlands Airport.

The plane, a Boeing 737, was reaching its cruising altitude when a blade broke off the left-hand engine. Severe vibrations were felt through the plane and smoke billowed into the cabin. There was a smell of burning. The plane prepared to make an emergency landing. As it approached the runway at East Midlands

from the east, the engine burst into flames.

The plane lost height and its tail crashed into the ground just east of the motorway. The plane bounced over the motorway and crashed into the western embankment next to the northerly carriageway and broke into three pieces. It was less than a quarter of a mile short of reaching the runway. A total of 47 people on board were killed and 79 others were injured. Perhaps remarkably, no one on the motorway was hurt and no vehicles were damaged.

The Kegworth air crash happened just two weeks after the Lockerbie disaster, when a Pan Am flight was blown up by a terrorist bomb. Although the circumstances of

Above: A crane lifts the Boeing 737's shattered tail section from the embankment onto the motorway to allow its removal.

Above: Upon impact, the aircraft broke into three sections.
Facing page: Rescue services search the remains of the Boeing 737.

Above: Gouges in the underside of the tail show where it hit the motorway before the plane slammed into the opposite embankment.

each disaster were very different, both events conspired to create a heightened sense of concern about the safety of air travel. In addition, Kegworth formed part of a catalogue of major civil disasters of the late 1980s (along with Hillsborough, the King's Cross fire, Piper Alpha, the *Herald of Free Enterprise* sinking and others), which some saw as evidence of a failure to take sufficient interest in health and safety in the 1980s.

The report into the Kegworth accident made 31 safety recommendations, including a revision of the brace position to be adopted by passengers in the event of a crash. Captain Kevin Hunt and his First Officer, David McClelland, who were both badly hurt in the accident,

were criticised for their actions and subsequently dismissed. Hunt spent some years in a wheelchair as a result of his injuries. McClelland was subsequently awarded £10,000 from British Midland Airways after bringing an unfair dismissal claim.

Despite criticism of the pilots in the official report, they were seen by many villagers in Kegworth as heroes for having avoided crashing the plane on their homes.

As you pass by the crash site on the M1 near East Midlands Airport there is nothing to mark where this happened, although there is a plaque on a motorway bridge nearby and a memorial to those who died and were injured in the village cemetery in Kegworth.

LINCOLN
RACECOURSE

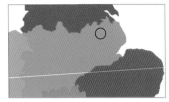

53° 13′ 56″ N, -0° 33′ 14″ E

21ST JULY, 1964

CARHOLME ROAD, LINCOLN, LN1 1SE

THE GRANDSTAND OF A RACECOURSE STILL THERE TO BE REOPENED

There is an unexpected sight for people driving into Lincoln on the A57 – a distinctive white racecourse sign and then a grandstand right next to the busy thoroughfare. Even though it closed more than 40 years ago, Lincoln Racecourse is still very visible to the passing traveller.

In fact, Lincoln Racecourse lives on in two ways. Firstly, its most famous race, the Lincoln Handicap, is still run at Doncaster, where it was transferred after the closure of Lincoln in 1964. Secondly, its grandstand is still there, used as a community facility. The grandstand is also the centrepiece of a plan by those who dream of reopening the course to resume racing in Lincoln.

Racing began in Lincoln in the 18th century on the course at Carholme to the west of the city. The most famous race held there each year was the Lincolnshire Handicap – traditionally held in March as a curtain raiser for the English flat racing season. Many famous horses ran at Lincoln including the legendary filly, Sceptre, in the 1902 Lincolnshire Handicap. The race often attracted large entries, including 57 for the 1948 race.

During the 1950s and 1960s Lincoln Racecourse struggled financially and in 1964 the Jockey Club decided not to sanction any more fixtures there. On 21st July, 1964 Lincoln Council announced its closure. The Lincolnshire, renamed the Lincoln Handicap, was taken over by Doncaster. The closure of Lincoln was one of a number of racecourse closures in the mid 1960s.

Curiously, the A57 road runs right through the course and was shut during race meetings. As well as the grandstand and the sign, some of the white fencing seen at racecourses is still there, but the area where the course was located has become much-loved common land.

The Lincoln Racecourse Regeneration Company has been trying to revive racing in Lincoln for a number of years. Their plans include the renovation of the grandstand and the reopening of the course for around 15 days a year. However, they have run into strong local opposition. In early 2012 there seemed very little prospect of the plans coming to fruition.

Sixty racecourses are still in operation in Britain in 2012, but many others have closed down over the past century. Most of those that closed have disappeared under redevelopment schemes, but Lincoln remains almost frozen in time.

Left: Lincoln racecourse in its heyday, seen from the grandstand. The 'runners and riders' structure, which still exists, can be seen at right.

Below: Lincoln's grandstand today, together with the old 'runners and riders' structure, which stand alongside the A57.

THE FIRST BUTLIN'S,
SKEGNESS

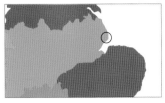

53° 10' 41" N, 0° 20' 59" E

11TH APRIL, 1936   BUTLIN'S RESORT, CHAPEL ST LEONARD'S ROAD, SKEGNESS, LINCOLNSHIRE, PE25 1NJ

BIRTHPLACE OF THE REDCOAT

Above: A Redcoat directs a new arrival to the swimming pool at Butlin's Skegness holiday camp in June 1947.

Above: Rows of original 1930s 'mock-Tudor' chalets at Skegness. Today,
one is preserved on the site as a listed building.
Below: The knobbly knees contest – a holidaymaker's favourite.

In time for Easter 1936 on the flatlands of Lincolnshire, one of the most enduring leisure brands of the 20th century was born. Sir Billy Butlin, a South African-born Briton, had first experienced summer camps when he lived in Canada as a teenager. The idea stayed with him and he realised it at Ingoldmells, near Skegness, where, more than 75 years later, after many reinventions, it is still going and entertaining almost 500,000 visitors a year.

Holiday camps weren't invented by Butlin, but it was he who is widely credited with turning them into a multi-million-pound industry, and it was the Skegness camp that kick-started the phenomenon. He had bought land at Ingoldmells in 1927 and opened an amusement park, which included a miniature railway and Britain's first dodgems. However, he had greater

Above: Bathing belles at Butlin's in June 1946, reopened after the war.
Top: A typical Butlin's advert, promising a holiday you wouldn't forget.

Above: Butlin's was designed to cater for everyone's needs on site. Why go to the beach when there was a big sand pit for the kids to play in?

Above: Holidaymakers enjoy a lunchtime drink in the large bar at the Skegness camp. Drinks had to be paid for, but all meals were included.

ambitions for the site and, after seeing the construction of the Warner's site at Seaton in Devon in 1935, he hired the same construction team to develop the Skegness site into his first holiday camp.

CAMP FOLLOWING

The original camp had 600 chalets with running water and electricity, 250 bathrooms, dining and entertainment halls, tennis courts, a theatre, a gym, a swimming pool and a boating lake. It cost £100,000 (about £5m at 2012 prices). Despite running short of money, and snow on the opening day, the camp was opened on schedule on 11th April, 1936. A week's stay cost between £2.05 and £3 (about £160 in 2012) for three meals a day including all entertainment. The first season proved successful and capacity at the camp had to be increased.

However, the key characteristic that has come to be associated with Butlin's, the Redcoat, was born out of Sir Billy's frustration with the way his visitors behaved. Apparently, the first visitors didn't get engaged with the facilities in the way he had hoped. Some of them were just sitting around and looking bored. So he asked

one of his team, Norman Bradford, a senior engineer on the site, to entertain them. He got up on stage, told a few jokes and encouraged the visitors to introduce themselves to each other.

The following day Butlin decided he needed an army of entertainers, who would all wear a distinctive uniform, which eventually became a red jacket. The Redcoat had been invented and the idea of communal jollity, which became the hallmark of Butlin's, was born. Comedians Dave Allen, Des O'Connor and Jimmy Tarbuck are just three famous names who started out as Butlin's Redcoats.

NAVAL BASE

During the Second World War, Butlin's Skegness was requisitioned and became HMS *Royal Arthur* – a naval training base. Despite being bombed many times, it was still in a good enough state at the end of the war to be handed back and reopened as a holiday camp in May 1946.

In the years since the war, the Butlin's site at Skegness has gone through many iterations. An airfield existed alongside the camp for many years. The hotel opened

Above: One of the many attractions of Butlin's Skegness camp was the large boating lake, complete with full-size boats.

Above: Holidaymakers enjoy the sun on the grass at Butlin's Skegness in June 1948. Instead of deckchairs there are moulded plastic seats.

alongside the camp was the first in Britain to have a television in 1948. A chairlift, a miniature railway and a monorail were all added in the 1960s.

MAJOR REVAMP

In 1987 there was a major revamp and the camp was rebranded as Funcoast World. New swimming pools were built, and many of the older buildings and original chalets were demolished. The miniature railway and the chairlift were removed. In the late 1990s, there was a further redevelopment, including the construction of the Skyline Pavilion.

The Butlin's brand was bought by Bourne Leisure Ltd from Rank in 2000. The monorail disappeared in 2002, but new attractions were added, including archery and rock climbing as what is now called Butlin's Resort, Skegness, adapted to new tastes. A new waterpark was due to open on the site in 2013. In 2011, the original 1936 Redcoat uniform was reintroduced to mark the 75th anniversary. One of the original chalets from 1936 is preserved on the site as a listed building in memory of the pioneering days of Sir Billy Butlin and his Redcoats.

Above: Happy campers sunbathe and cool off by taking a dip in the swimming pool at Butlin's Skegness in June 1948.

FLIXBOROUGH
DISASTER

53° 37' 25" N, -0° 41' 49" E

1ST JUNE, 1974   FLIXBOROUGH INDUSTRIAL ESTATE, FLIXBOROUGH, NORTH LINCOLNSHIRE, DN15 8SH

Above: A local resident's car destroyed by the blast from the explosion at the Nypro plant at Flixborough. In the background smoke billows into the air as the factory continues to burn.

THE BIGGEST PEACETIME EXPLOSION IN 20TH CENTURY BRITAIN

People who live near industrial sites live with the fear that one day something awful will happen. Often communities close to industrial plants harbour suspicions that what goes on inside these places is fundamentally unsafe. Usually, their fears are misguided, but every so often industrial processes go wrong and the worst does happen. One such occasion occurred on Saturday, 1st June, 1974, close to the village of Flixborough near Scunthorpe in North Lincolnshire.

The Nypro plant produced caprolactam, a chemical used in the manufacture of nylon. The process involved the use of six reactors. Two months prior to the explosion, a crack was discovered in one of the reactors. It was decided to put a temporary pipe in place to create a diversion round the damaged reactor so that production could continue while repairs were carried out.

Just before five o'clock that afternoon, the temporary pipe ruptured and 40 tonnes of cyclohexane leaked out, formed a vapour cloud and exploded when the cloud came into contact with an ignition source. The Nypro plant was totally destroyed, killing 28 people, including all 18 working in the control room, nine other workers on the site and a delivery driver who suffered a heart attack.

Above: Firefighters arrive to be greeted by dense black clouds of smoke and towering flames. Some fires burned for ten days after the explosion.

Above: An aerial view of the devastated Nypro plant. Had the explosion occurred on a weekday, as many as 500 could have been killed.

There was structural damage as far as eight miles away and the explosion was heard 30 miles away. It was the biggest peacetime explosion in Britain until the Buncefield explosion in Hertfordshire in 2005. The pall of smoke drifted for miles across the Humber Estuary and beyond. The explosion was graphically captured by television because both the BBC and ITV had crews nearby covering the annual Appleby-Frodingham gala.

FAULTY PIPE

The official inquiry found serious faults in the way the temporary pipe had been installed around the damaged reactor. Flixborough led to a tightening of the rules about procedures for the use of hazardous substances in industrial processes. Years after the disaster, alternative theories of why it happened were advanced and there were unproven allegations of a cover-up of the true facts.

Despite the scale of the destruction, and in the face of local opposition, the plant was rebuilt, but only survived a few more years before a downturn in the market for nylon forced its closure. The factory was demolished in 1981 and the site is now occupied by an industrial estate and a power station. A memorial to those who died in the explosion was erected in front of the rebuilt factory in 1977 and then moved to the local churchyard after the factory's closure. However, part of it was stolen and only the plinth remains, but it does include the names of those who died.

THE SCARBOROUGH
BLITZ

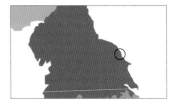

54° 16' 30" N, -0° 24' 52" E

SCARBOROUGH, NORTH YORKSHIRE

GERMAN SHELLING OF AN ENGLISH SEASIDE RESORT

On the morning of Wednesday 16th December, 1914, the house at 22 Westbourne Park, Scarborough, took a direct hit when two German warships lying about 600 yards off the beach began shelling the town. A 14-month-old boy, John Shields Ryalls, was among those killed. He was one of 17 victims of the attack on the seaside resort by the Imperial German Navy, just four months into the First World War.

The raid lasted about an hour and many buildings in the town were hit, including the Coastguard station, the castle, some churches and a number of private houses. There was considerable panic as people fled into the neighbouring countryside and scrambled to board trains to Leeds and elsewhere.

ACT OF REVENGE

The attack marked the most violent day in the history of the grand old Yorkshire resort and remains one of the most curious episodes of the First World War. It is still not clear quite why the Germans attacked Scarborough, or indeed neighbouring Whitby later that day. Neither town was of military significance, although the Germans also shelled Hartlepool, which did have an important military role, on the same day.

Prior to the raid on Scarborough, the two warships involved – the SMS *Derfflinger* and the SMS *Von der Tann* – had been part of a cat-and-mouse game involving the German and British navies in the North Sea. One German admiral later described the attack on Scarborough as an act of revenge for the defeat inflicted on the Germans by the Royal Navy in the Battle of the Falkland Islands in the South Atlantic a week earlier. After the raid, there was criticism of the Royal Navy for its failure to prevent the attack.

DEATH TOLL

In total, 137 people were killed and 592 injured in the raids on the three towns that day. Whatever the intended consequences, one definite effect was a boost in recruitment to the British armed forces. There was a widespread feeling that the Germans had broken the rules of war by attacking a largely defenceless and militarily unimportant place. "Remember Scarborough – Enlist Now" became the recruiting motto immediately after the raid and an increase in people signing up to fight was reported.

Number 22 Westbourne Park and most other buildings hit in the raid, were rebuilt. There is no memorial in Scarborough to the bombardment, although the victims are included on a war memorial in the town. However, as the centenary of the raid approached, there were plans to mark the most famous moment in the town's history.

Above: A grocer's shop in Scarborough, its plate-glass windows and fascia smashed by the German shelling of the town.

Left: The ruins of Number 2 Wykeham Street in Scarborough, where three people died when a German shell smashed into it and exploded. One of them was Albert Bennett, the only soldier to be killed in the raid.

Far left: The lighthouse on Vincent's Pier, Scarborough, was also hit and so badly damaged that it had to be demolished.

SCARBOROUGH HOTEL
LANDSLIDE

54° 15' 57" N, -0° 23' 38" E

Above: Men and equipment move onto the Holbeck Hall Hotel site ready to demolish the remainder of the structure.

THE HOTEL THAT SLID INTO THE SEA

For several days in early June 1993, the country – indeed the world – was gripped by the drama of a hotel perched on a cliff above Scarborough slipping into the sea. Newsdesks everywhere loved the pictures and the metaphors were flowing. For many local people, this epitomised Scarborough's slow slide from its former splendour as a premier seaside resort. Nationally, some commentators managed to turn the demise of Holbeck Hall into a metaphor for the country's decline.

Holbeck Hall Hotel had been built in 1879. Set in spacious grounds on the cliffs above the South Bay, it was regarded as one of the top hotels in Scarborough. At the time of its collapse, it was the only four-star hotel in the town. People still flocked there for a genteel offering reminiscent of a former age. The hotel, along with some others in Scarborough, was owned by Barry and Joan Turner, who believed that the Yorkshire resort had the potential to relive former glories and pull in people wanting an elegant place to stay.

On 3rd June, 1993, a landslide began beneath the hotel. By the 5th June, after heavy rain, parts of the hotel had collapsed and fallen into the sea. Later the rest of the hotel had to be demolished. The explanation appears to have been that heavy rainfall in the months before had saturated the cliffside, which had been fissured by two earlier dry summers. The ground was literally taken from under the hotel. Joan Turner said at the time that she had lost her dream.

The world's media gathered in large numbers and the images of a part of Scarborough's seaside heritage slipping into the sea transfixed television audiences everywhere. The collapse became a tourist attraction in its own right for a few days.

COASTAL EROSION

The Holbeck Hall collapse was just one example of the phenomenon of coastal erosion which was, and still is, a significant problem for much of the eastern coastline of Britain. Many other parts of the Yorkshire coast as well as the East Anglian and Lincolnshire coasts have been affected. Although substantial sea defences have been put in place in some areas, the financial reality is that, for many stretches of coastline, it is simply not affordable to provide protection from coastal erosion and landslips.

Nevertheless, the collapse of Holbeck Hall led to a landmark legal case in 2000, when the owners of the hotel sued Scarborough Borough Council, alleging that they had been negligent in failing to take measures to prevent the landslip. The case was unsuccessful, with the court ruling that the Council could not be held responsible for the causes of the landslip and was not therefore liable.

The site where Holbeck Hall stood remains fenced off and empty almost 20 years after its demise.

Above: A large section of the hotel's roof crashes to the ground as the unstable cliff continues to collapse.

Below: An aerial view of the massive landslip on the cliffs at Scarborough, showing the hotel only feet from the edge.

AYRESOME PARK
MIDDLESBROUGH

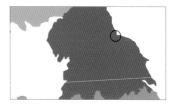

54° 33' 51" N, 1° 14' 48" W

19TH JULY, 1966

AYRESOME PARK ESTATE, MIDDLESBROUGH, TS5 6BU

WHERE THE NORTH KOREAN FOOTBALL TEAM HUMBLED MIGHTY ITALY

Above: Middlesbrough's Ayresome Park ground in September 1975.
It had been the team's home since 1903.

Of the eight football grounds used when England hosted and won the World Cup in the summer of 1966, only four of them remain – Everton's Goodison Park, Manchester United's Old Trafford, Villa Park, Birmingham, and Hillsborough, Sheffield. The others, Ayresome Park, Middlesbrough, along with Roker Park, Sunderland, White City, London and the original Wembley have since been demolished. Ayresome Park is probably the most romantic of these because it is mainly remembered for the most remarkable game of the tournament, apart from the final.

In fact, Ayresome Park wasn't supposed to stage World Cup matches at all. The original intention had been to use Newcastle United's St James's Park ground, but a dispute between the club and Newcastle City Council prevented that and, relatively late in the process in 1964, Ayresome Park was added to the list. There were some hurried ground improvements, including a new roof on the East Stand and around 7,500 seats

installed on what had previously been terracing.

It was on the evening of Tuesday, 19th July, 1966 that sporting history was made. It was a Group 4 match between Italy, one of the favourites, and North Korea. The latter, 1000–1 outsiders going into the tournament, had already played twice at Ayresome Park and had won the affections of the local crowd. In their previous matches they had lost to the Soviet Union, the eventual group winners, but had drawn with Chile. Italy came into the match having beaten Chile, but having lost to the Soviet Union.

Attendances at all three games at Ayresome Park were disappointing and only 18,727 fans were there to see North Korea pull off the shock of the competition. Pak Doo-Ik scored the only goal of the game just before half time to take them into the Quarter-Finals and send the mighty Italians out of the tournament. The black-and-white television coverage of the match shows the standing ovation given to the North Koreans who became the heroes of the tournament. There was

Above: Chile press home an attack against North Korea during the 1966 World Cup Group 4 first-round match at Ayresome Park. They drew 1-1.

Above: A British sailor shares in the joy of the North Koreans after they beat favourites Italy 1-0 by lifting the arm of goal scorer Pak Doo-Ik.

enormous support across the country for the North Koreans when they played in the Quarter-Finals. A further shock appeared to be on the cards when they took a 3–0 lead against Portugal at Goodison Park, but they eventually lost 5–3.

HEYDAY TO DECLINE

The 1966 World Cup was probably the highpoint of the history of Ayresome Park. Middlesbrough had moved there in 1903 when they were elected to the Football League. The highest attendance was a Christmas derby match against arch-rivals Newcastle United in 1949. The stadium was graced by such stars as Wilf Mannion, who played 368 times for the club between 1936 and

1954, and George Hardwick – both highly-regarded England internationals. Brian Clough, later to be one of the most successful English football managers, played for Middlesbrough during the 1950s. During most of their 92 years at Ayresome Park Middlesbrough were rarely out of the top two divisions of English football and in the late 1930s were regarded as a potentially championship winning team.

The demise of Ayresome Park in the 1990s was a direct consequence of the Taylor Report into the safety of stadia that followed the Hillsborough Disaster in 1989. Faced with a requirement to have all-seater stadia in the top divisions, Middlesbrough had a dilemma. Their traditional home was crammed into the middle of a residential area with no room to expand. Had they redeveloped Ayresome Park as an all-seater stadium, the capacity would have been limited to 20,000. So they took the decision to move and, with help from Teesside Development Corporation, they relocated to the new Riverside Stadium in 1995.

THE LAST MATCH

The last competitive match at Ayresome Park took place on 30th April, 1995 when Middlesbrough beat Luton Town 2–1 to secure the Division One title and promotion to the Premier League. Ayresome Park was used as a training ground for a further season, but was demolished in 1997. The site is now a housing estate, although part of the Holgate-end wall remained within the new estate and was repaired in late 2011. The gates from Ayresome Park were re-erected at the Riverside Stadium.

Middlesbrough's move from Ayresome Park to the Riverside Stadium was one of the first in what started as a trickle and then became a wave of relocations of British football clubs. These moves were prompted partly by safety, but also by footballing egos. The desire to have shiny new stadia was often part of the plan of the new breed of football owners. In most cases the relocations took stadia away from their traditional city-centre or inner-city locations to venues with better parking and other facilities. The football ground sandwiched in the middle of working-class terraced streets has been replaced by the stadium alongside the out-of-town retail park.

An appropriate postscript to the story of Ayresome Park took place in 2002 when seven surviving members of the North Korean team, who'd beaten Italy back in 1966, returned to Middlesbrough and were warmly received on the pitch at the Riverside Stadium.

Left: A 1966 World Cup ticketing information booklet, giving details of tickets and prices, together with the application process.

Above: A 1966 World Cup commemorative four-penny stamp issued by the Post Office in advance of the tournament. Subsequently, the same stamp was re-issued with the words "ENGLAND WINNERS" added.

SUNDERLAND'S BYGONE
SHIPYARDS

54° 54' 42" N, 1° 22' 25" W

7TH DECEMBER, 1988   UNIVERSITY OF SUNDERLAND, SR6 0DD AND OTHER ADDRESSES

Above: Behind a network of scaffolding, the hull of a ship is assembled in this shipyard on the Wear in 1910.

Above: A hive of activity on the banks of the River Wear in Sunderland in 1910. This was the heyday of the industry in Sunderland.

ONCE THE HOME OF A MIGHTY INDUSTRY

Recalling places where news was made should not just be confined to the locations of specific events or individual incidents that made headlines. It's also about the marking of trends, the comings and goings of social, political, cultural and industrial phenomena.

Looking along the banks of the River Wear in Sunderland, there are now few clues that this was once a bustling centre of heavy industry. At its height, the shipbuilding industry of Sunderland was an industrial powerhouse producing vessels that went to all corners of the globe. Now there is virtually no discernible trace of the industry that was once the focal point and *raison d'être* for Sunderland's existence.

Shipbuilding on the River Wear is thought to date back to 1346, when the first shipyard opened in the Hendon area of the city. Between then and the termination of shipbuilding more than 600 years later, there are estimated to have been more than 400 registered shipyards in Sunderland. Swan Hunter, Pickersgill's, Doxford and Sons, and Short Brothers are just some of the famous names to have occupied the banks of the Wear.

Although shipbuilding suffered regular depressions

as demand rose and fell, the late 19th and early 20th centuries were the heyday of the industry on the Wear. More than 12,000 people were employed in shipbuilding in Sunderland at the height of the industry. In 1906, the busiest year in the industry's history, 97 vessels were produced in Sunderland in a single year.

After the Second World War, international competition increased and gradually the industry on Wearside reduced. In 1977, what remained of the British shipbuilding industry was nationalised. The two remaining yards in Sunderland merged in 1980, but the end came on 7th December, 1988, when the last remaining yard, then named North-East Shipbuilders, closed, bringing to an end the industry that had for so long been Sunderland's most famous export.

Now the banks of the Wear are quiet, although two ship repair businesses still exist in the town. The areas once occupied by the shipyards have been put to a variety of uses. The University of Sunderland, which grew out of Sunderland Polytechnic, has developed its campuses and halls of residence along both banks of the river. The National Glass Centre sits on the site of the former J.L.Thompson and Sons yard. There are various business and retail parks, and there is a riverside sculpture project that recalls the industry. Sunderland Museum contains some relics and memorabilia of the industry, but most traces of shipbuilding have disappeared.

Sunderland has remained an industrial centre. In 1986, just as shipbuilding was disappearing, Nissan opened what is now the largest car factory in Britain on the site of the old Sunderland airfield.

Below: The scene from Sunderland Bridge in July 1947, showing Austin's shipyard in the right foreground and Bartrams behind.

Below: The view from Sunderland Bridge today. The once mighty industry is no more and the riverside is quiet.

NEWCASTLE'S
VICTORIA
TUNNEL

54° 58' 21" N, 1° 35' 23" W

1939–1945   VICTORIA TUNNEL ENTRANCE, OUSE STREET, NEWCASTLE UPON TYNE, NE1 2PA

Above: The entrance to the Victoria Tunnel in 1939, when it was being converted into an air-raid shelter capable of housing thousands.

Above: The modern entrance to the Victoria Tunnel, with boards showing a map of its extent and giving interesting facts about it.

FORMER MINING TUNNEL TURNED INTO
A WARTIME AIR-RAID SHELTER

The standard images of people sheltering below ground during air-raids in the Second World War often feature the London Underground. Of course, many British cities other than London suffered heavy bombing and their residents all needed protection from air-raids. One of the largest underground shelters in Britain was in Newcastle upon Tyne.

The Victoria Tunnel had been built between 1839 and 1842 to transport coal from the Spital Tongues Colliery on the north side of Newcastle to the River Tyne. This subterranean wagonway was a much more efficient way of getting coal from the mine to the waterside to be loaded onto barges on the Tyne than the previous method of taking it through the streets. There was a gradual downward gradient to the river so the coal wagons were able to roll down to the port. A rope was attached to the last wagon and the wagons were towed back to the mine by a stationary steam engine.

Above: An illuminated section of the Victoria Tunnel close to the Ouse Street entrance, allowing guided tours to take place.

The wagonway was deemed a success and is said to have reduced the pit's transport costs by almost 90 per cent. However, the tunnel's life as a colliery wagonway was short-lived. The colliery went out of business in 1860 and the tunnel was closed. Over the next 80 years it was largely forgotten although part of it was used briefly in the late 1920s as a mushroom farm.

However, at the outbreak of war in 1939, the tunnel was brought back into use and converted into an air-raid shelter. £37,000 (around £1.8m at 2012 prices) was spent to provide seating for over 5,000 people and bunk beds for 500. The tunnel was cleaned of coal dust. Parts of the walls were whitewashed. Blast walls were constructed to deflect any bomb debris that might reach the tunnel. Chemical toilets were provided and there was electric lighting. There were seven entrances along the two-mile length of the tunnel.

The tunnel was just seven feet high and about six feet wide. At its deepest point, it was 85 feet below the surface. Those who sheltered there during the war say it was dark, damp and uncomfortable, but people kept their spirits up with singing and gossiping. When the war ended most of the fittings were removed and the tunnel was again closed.

During the 1950s, the tunnel was considered as a bunker in the event of nuclear attack. In 1976 part of it was converted into a sewer, but around a third of the length of the tunnel remained. In 2006 work was carried out to make the tunnel properly accessible again, and in 2009 tours were started. The Ouseburn Trust now runs five guided tours each week throughout the year to enable people to relive this slice of wartime history.

EDINBURGH'S
ELEPHANT HOUSE
CAFÉ

55° 56' 50" N, 3° 11' 29" W

1990s

21 GEORGE IV BRIDGE, EDINBURGH, EH1 1EN.

WHERE J.K. ROWLING WROTE THE FIRST HARRY POTTER NOVEL

Above: The interior of The Elephant House, one of Edinburgh's most well-known coffee shops thanks to the J.K. Rowling connection.

There's something particularly romantic about imagining people who have yet to do the thing for which they will become well-known going about their business anonymously in the days before they become famous. The story of J.K. Rowling writing the first Harry Potter novel in an Edinburgh café fits this idea perfectly.

It's impossible not to be moved by the story of a single parent and would-be author, who spends her time in cafés to save on heating bills in her flat, producing what proves to be one of the most successful children's literary phenomena of the 20th century in the warmth of an Edinburgh coffee house. This account of the birth of the Harry Potter novels contains an element of truth, and The Elephant House café in the centre of Edinburgh has, not surprisingly, made the most of its connections with J.K. Rowling. The truth, not unexpectedly, is a little different.

J.K. Rowling did indeed frequent The Elephant House when she was writing the first Harry Potter novel and she was a single parent at the time, after the break-up of her first marriage. The Elephant House was one of several Edinburgh cafés she used during that period of her life, although she has refuted the idea that she had no heating in her flat. Her rather more prosaic explanation is that she wrote in cafés because going out for walks was the best way to get her baby to sleep.

WIZARD IDEA

The Harry Potter story began earlier and well away from Edinburgh. Rowling was brought up in Gloucestershire, went to university in Exeter and worked for Amnesty International in London before moving to Manchester. According to her own account, it was when she was on a train journey between Manchester and London in 1990 that she first had the idea. In 1992 she married in Portugal, where she had moved to teach English as

a foreign language, and her daughter was born the following year. However, her marriage ended the same year and she moved back to Britain and went to live in Edinburgh to be near her sister. Living on benefits during the period from 1993 to 1995, she completed the first novel *Harry Potter and the Philosopher's Stone*, which, after being rejected by many publishers, was published in 1997.

Six further Harry Potter novels followed and a series of films based on the books. More than 400 million copies of the novels have been sold worldwide, and Rowling was said to be the 12th richest woman in Britain in 2008.

The Elephant House café has Potter memorabilia on its walls and references to other famous authors who have worked there. There are even messages from customers to J.K. Rowling in the toilets! The author has acknowledged the role the café played in the early years of her writing career. Rowling revealed in 2008 that she had returned to Edinburgh cafés to work on new writing projects.

Above: J.K. Rowling at a book signing. Her immensely popular series of Harry Potter novels has made her a multi-millionaire.

Right: The Elephant House café on George IV Bridge in the heart of Edinburgh.

SCAPA
FLOW

58° 50' 30" N, 3° 12' 41" W

21st JUNE, 1919

SCAPA FLOW VISITORS CENTRE, LYNESS, HOY, ORKNEY, KW16 3NU

THE SCENE OF THE GREATEST NAVAL SCUTTLING OF ALL TIME

Above: Royal Naval warships shelter in Scapa Flow in June 1917. Kite balloons are flown to provide protection from low-level air attack.

It is hard to imagine what a hive of activity Scapa Flow would have been during both world wars. In the 21st century, it is a relatively quiet spot beloved of scuba divers in search of wrecks, although still an important base for the oil industry. But between 1914 and 1918, and then again from 1939 to 1945, it made a major contribution to the war effort. It deserves its reputation as one of the most significant locations in naval history.

Scapa Flow is one of the great natural harbours of the world. It is relatively sheltered, lying between Orkney and a number of adjacent islands. Its advantages as a natural harbour were recognised as long ago as the time of the Vikings, but it was at the beginning of the First World War that it began its role as Britain's main wartime naval base. Before that, the Royal Navy's main bases were in the south, facing the traditional enemies of France and Spain. However, it was recognised that a northern base was needed to command the North Sea and be able to face the threat posed by the German High Seas Fleet. Scapa Flow had been used for naval exercises before the First World War, but by the time of the outbreak of war, it had been chosen ahead of other possible locations even though it wasn't properly fortified.

During the First World War, Scapa Flow served as a safe base for the Royal Navy. It had been fortified with minefields and barriers, and two attempted German attacks were unsuccessful.

However, the most dramatic event at Scapa Flow related to the First World War occurred once the armistice had been signed. After Germany's defeat, 74 German ships were held there while discussions continued about their fate at the Versailles peace talks.

Above: The German battle cruiser SMS Hindenburg is salvaged at Scapa Flow. Commissioned in 1917, the ship saw little action before being interned in the Orkneys. She was the last German ship to sink there.

Above left: A scuttled First World War German destroyer is raised from the depths of Scapa Flow in May 1926. Most of the sunken vessels were salvaged in this manner.

Left: The remains of a block ship in the sound between Burray and Glimps Holm. Such vessels were sunk in a number of channels between the Orkney Islands during the First World War to deny access to enemy vessels, such as submarines.

Above: Churchill Barrier No. 3, connecting Glimps Holm (foreground) with the island of Burray. The barriers act as causeways today.

However, on 21st June, 1919, the commander of the German ships, Rear Admiral Ludwig von Reuter, decided to scuttle the fleet to prevent them from falling into the hands of the victorious allies.

The scuttling happened after much of the British fleet had left Scapa Flow on exercises. Frantic attempts were made by the British to prevent the sinkings, but in total 52 of the 74 ships were lost. More than a thousand German sailors abandoned their ships and were picked up and treated as prisoners of war.

At first most of the scuttled ships were left in Scapa Flow, as it was deemed to be too expensive to salvage them, but in 1923 a salvage operation was begun after local people complained that the wrecks were a hazard to navigation. Eventually, an entrepreneur, Ernest Cox,

became involved and his company managed to salvage 45 of the 52 ships over the next 15 years. Indeed, his operation was only halted by the outbreak of the Second World War.

VULNERABILITY

Scapa Flow was again chosen as the northern base for the Royal Navy in 1939. However, the defences from the First World War had fallen into disrepair and the base's vulnerability was evident early in the war when a German submarine penetrated the harbour in October and sank HMS *Royal Oak* with the loss of over 800 lives. A German air-raid three days later damaged another ship.

Above: The remainder of the sunken German ships, together with the block ships, provide sport divers with a fascinating seascape to explore.

Defences were improved with minefields, booms and, most famously, four barriers blocking the eastern approaches, which became known as the 'Churchill Barriers'. These were built using Italian prisoners of war, possibly in contravention of the Geneva Convention. Scapa Flow proved to be a largely secure base of operations for the Navy throughout the war.

The Lyness Naval Base was closed in 1957 and an era in naval history came to an end. The Churchill Barriers are still there, used as roads linking the various islands of Orkney. Scapa Flow plays a role in the oil industry, with tankers using the waters while loading at the Flotta Oil Terminal and also for ship-to-ship transfers. The Golden Wharf, a massive pier built during the Second World War, has recently been redeveloped and is a focus for the emerging marine and tidal-energy sector.

SURVIVING RELICS

A number of the wartime buildings that formed part of the base survive, including the pumphouse and one of the huge surface oil storage tanks, which now house the Scapa Flow Visitor Centre and Museum. Six underground oil storage tanks, capable of holding more than 100,000 tons of oil, remain in the hill above Lyness.

Scapa Flow is still ringed by the remains of its defences, the most visible of which are the coastal batteries at Hoxa Head and Stanger Head, guarding the main entrance to the Flow. All other remains of the naval base are no more, except for the wrecks below the surface. The British ships sunk there are designated as war graves, but the seven remaining scuttled German ships from the First World War are of great interest to divers.

INVERNESS

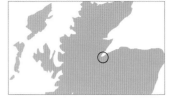

FORMULA

7TH SEPTEMBER, 1921   INVERNESS TOWN HOUSE, HIGH STREET, INVERNESS, IV1 1JJ

THE FIRST BRITISH CABINET MEETING OUTSIDE LONDON

Above: Prime Minister David Lloyd George (L) with King George V (R) and Alfred Donald Mackintosh, Lord Lieutenant of Inverness, at Moy House, Inverness in September 1921.

Above: Prime Minister David Lloyd George leaves Inverness Town House after the historic Cabinet meeting that led to the creation of the Irish Free State.

Holding meetings of the British Cabinet away from 10 Downing Street in London no longer seems remarkable in the 21st century. Indeed, it has become rather fashionable since Gordon Brown reintroduced the idea in 2008. In 1921, however, this was quite a radical concept, and the meeting in Inverness was the first and remained the only Cabinet meeting outside London for the best part of a century.

The reason this historic event took place in Inverness was that the Prime Minister, David Lloyd George, was on holiday at Gairloch in Wester Ross when he heard that Southern Ireland wished to break away from the British Crown. His deputy was at Beaufort Castle and the King was also in Scotland – at Moy House. Instead of returning to London, he called the Cabinet to Inverness and they met at 11 o'clock on the morning of Wednesday, 7th September, 1921 at the Inverness Town House.

The discussions that took place during the meeting produced what became known as the 'Inverness Formula'. This formed the basis for the negotiations that led to the treaty establishing the Irish Free State.

The members of the Cabinet, which included two future prime ministers, Stanley Baldwin and Winston Churchill, all signed a blank sheet of paper passed around during the meeting as a record of attendance. The paper is still preserved in Inverness by the local council.

Inverness Town House had been built between 1878 and 1882, and it served as the headquarters of the local council until the 1990s. It remains an imposing building in the centre of the town used by a number of council services as well as being a venue for meetings, civic events, concerts and marriages.

DUNBLANE SCHOOL
MASSACRE

56° 11' 25" N, 3° 58' 27" W

13TH MARCH, 1996   DUNBLANE PRIMARY SCHOOL, DOUNE ROAD, DUNBLANE, STIRLING, FK15 9AU

GUNMAN OPENS FIRE ON CHILDREN AND THEN KILLS HIMSELF

Above: A chillingly disarming photograph of gunman Thomas Hamilton.

Right: A policeman watches over the gymnasium where 16 children and their teacher were gunned down.

Dunblane is a well-to-do community of around 8,000 people in the central belt of Scotland near Stirling. It has a cathedral and calls itself a city. Outside of Scotland, most people would not have heard of it until the morning of Wednesday, 13th March, 1996, since which time the name 'Dunblane' has forever been associated with massacres and firearms.

Indiscriminate shooting sprees are mercifully rare in Britain and it is invidious to compare tragedies. But the fact that most of the victims were small children marks the Dunblane massacre as one of the most terrible events outside of wartime in 20th-century Britain.

Just after 9.30 that morning, Thomas Hamilton walked into Dunblane Primary School in Doune Road in the town carrying four loaded weapons, all of which he held legally. He went to the school's gym and opened fire on a class of five- and six-year-old children. Sixteen children and their teacher died as a result of the attack. Hamilton left the gym and fired at children in a mobile classroom and in the direction of a corridor before returning to the gym and shooting himself.

His motives have never been definitively established. He was an out-of-work shopkeeper who had previously been a Scout leader. He was known to the police as a result of complaints of inappropriate behaviour towards young boys. His Scout warrant had been withdrawn in the 1970s. Immediately prior to the shooting he had complained to several MPs and to the Queen that he was being persecuted over his attempts to set up a boys' club. In the years since the massacre, there has been a series of claims about Central Scotland Police's alleged failure to have understood the threat posed by Hamilton prior to the shooting.

FIREARM RESTRICTIONS

In the immediate aftermath of the Dunblane shooting there were widespread calls for restrictions on gun ownership. A series of campaigns and petitions led to the introduction of restrictions on ownership of firearms, which were further strengthened after the election of the Labour Government in 1997. The official inquiry into Dunblane also recommended tighter security in schools and various measures were also introduced.

The gym where the massacre took place was demolished a month after the shooting and replaced with a small garden with a plaque bearing the names of the victims. In 1998 the whole of Dunblane Primary School was substantially refurbished.

There are also memorials in the town's cemetery and in Dunblane Cathedral. In 2004 a new youth and community centre, the Dunblane Centre, was built in part from funds sent by well-wishers following the shooting. Psychological support was provided in the town for many years after the shooting.

Dunblane is a commuter town with quite a high turnover of population. Although many people directly affected by the shootings still live there, many new people have come into the town since 1996. There is a strong sense of a community that remembers, but that has come to terms with the most violent episode in its history.

Tennis player Andy Murray, who was brought up in Dunblane, was eight and a pupil at the school at the time of the massacre. Murray's family still live in the town and residents say they are glad that his fame as a tennis player has given people another reason to know of Dunblane.

Above: The memorial stone commemorating the murdered children in the cathedral in Dunblane.

Above: Two children read the messages of condolence at the impromptu floral tribute to the murdered children and their teacher at Dunblane Primary School.

CASE OF THE
SNAIL
IN THE BOTTLE

55° 50' 36" N, 4° 25' 56" W

26TH AUGUST, 1928   CORNER OF WELLMEADOW STREET AND LADY LANE, PAISLEY, RENFREWSHIRE, PA1 2EF

SNAIL IN GINGER BEER THAT LED TO A LANDMARK LEGAL RULING

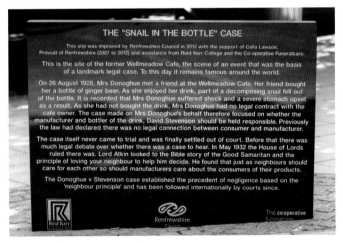

Above: A commorative plaque that stands on the site of the Wellmeadow Café and describes the landmark 'Snail in the Bottle' case.

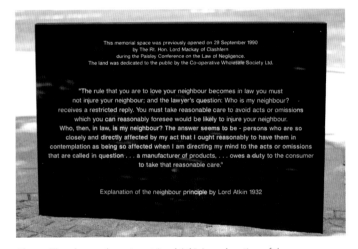

Above: The plaque also sets out Lord Atkin's explanation of the neighbour principle under which the case was brought in 1932.

On the evening of Sunday, 26th August, 1928, at around 9pm, May Donoghue met a friend in a café in Wellmeadow Street in Paisley, near Glasgow. Her friend ordered two drinks and, it is alleged, a decomposing snail was discovered in the bottle when the drink, probably a ginger beer, was poured. Later May Donoghue complained of stomach pains and a doctor diagnosed gastroenteritis.

The following April, May Donoghue brought a case against the manufacturer of the drink, David Stevenson. Her solicitor was Walter Leechman, who had already brought other cases against drinks manufacturers. Donoghue claimed £500 damages for the illness and the upset caused by the incident.

What then followed was a lengthy legal process that took four years to complete, but which resulted in a ruling that remains one of the most far-reaching in legal history. Previously, May Donoghue, who hadn't bought the drink herself, and who had no contract with the café owner or the manufacturer, could not have established any responsibility towards her by the manufacturer. The law only recognised such a duty of care in certain limited circumstances.

When the House of Lords finally ruled on the case in 1932, they voted by 3–2 that there was such a duty of care by the manufacturer to the ultimate consumer on the basis of what was called the 'neighbour principle'. This was an important extension of the law of tort and May Donoghue was given leave to pursue the case.

In the end the precise facts were never established in court because Stevenson died before the case was heard and his executors settled out of court, paying £200 damages. There are suspicions that the whole case may have been set up to test the legal position.

The café where the landmark case originated at the junction of Wellmeadow Street and Lady Lane is no longer there. However, such is the worldwide legal interest in the case that a commemorative bench and plaque mark the spot where the café once stood. In May 2012, to mark the 80th anniversary of the ruling, an international legal conference was held in Paisley to discuss the history and significance of the case.

Above: Civic dignitaries and lawyers attending the 80th-anniversary conference honouring the Paisley snail march to the memorial site.

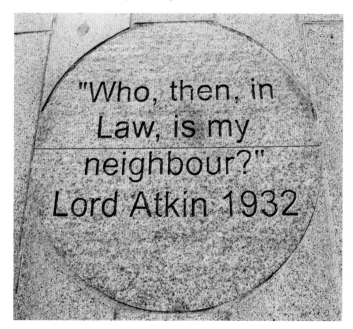

Above: A quote concerning the neighbour principle from Lord Atkin in 1932, carved on a stone and set in the paving at the memorial site.

Above: The new plaque commemorating the landmark legal case was unveiled by Ellen Farmer of the Old Paisley Society on 25th May, 2012.

LOCKERBIE BOMBING

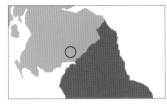

55° 6' 56" N, 3° 21' 26" W

21ST DECEMBER, 1988   SHERWOOD CRESCENT, LOCKERBIE, DUMFRIES AND GALLOWAY, DG11 2DY

BRITAIN'S WORST TERRORIST ATTACK

Above: The nose of the Pan Am jet, including the cockpit, lies shattered in a field. The aircraft disintegrated within seconds of the explosion.

Sherwood Crescent is a quiet residential street near the main A74(M) road on the outskirts of the small market town of Lockerbie. Like so many other places where tragedy has struck, the overwhelming impression is of ordinariness. However, the tell-tale sign is the age of the houses. They are new because a large part of the street was demolished and rebuilt after the events of Wednesday, 21st December, 1988, when Britain's worst terrorist incident was visited on this quiet Scottish community.

The blowing up of a plane just four days before Christmas, killing everyone on board, would have constituted a crime of such enormity in any event. However, the tragedy was magnified and compounded by the pure chance that the wreckage quite literally fell out of the sky and landed on houses where families were preparing for Christmas. Had the explosion happened a few seconds earlier or later, then Lockerbie might have been spared.

Flight Pan Am 103, a Boeing 747, took off from London Heathrow Airport just before 6.30pm bound for New York JFK Airport. It was flying at 31,000 feet when, just after 7pm it disappeared off radar screens and contact was lost. An explosion had made a hole

Above: Police and accident investigators discuss the situation against a backdrop of badly damaged houses in Lockerbie.

Above: Only the walls of these bungalows were left standing after the explosion of the wreckage of Pan Am's Flight 103.

Below: The huge crater gouged out of the earth next to the A47(M), caused by the jet's wing section as it slammed into the ground at 500mph.

Below: Police officers stand guard over a large section of wreckage from the doomed airliner. More than 10,000 items of debris were retrieved.

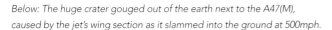

18 inches wide in the fuselage. It is believed the plane broke into at least three pieces within a few seconds of the explosion. The wreckage plunged earthward.

Less than one minute after the explosion, a large section of the fuselage landed on Sherwood Crescent at an estimated speed of 500mph, where it ignited destroying several houses and damaging many others. A crater almost 165 feet wide opened up. Another section of fuselage landed on a house in Park Place, although the occupant survived. The cockpit landed in a field at the nearby village of Tundergarth. Debris, bodies and personal effects were strewn all over the area. All 259 people on board the plane, including the 16 crew, were killed and 11 residents of Sherwood Close also died.

The investigation, the criminal proceedings that followed and the political ramifications of Lockerbie have continued ever since. It wasn't until 2001 that Libyan Abdelbaset-al-Megrahi was convicted of murder and sentenced to life imprisonment at a special Scottish Court sitting in the Netherlands. In 2009 al-Megrahi was released on compassionate grounds by the Scottish Government after doctors diagnosed him with terminal cancer. He died in May 2012.

Above: New homes have been built on the site of the devastation in Lockerbie, together with a memorial garden.

Below: A CIA analysis detailing claims of responsibility for the bombing by various organisations immediately after the atrocity.

CENTRAL INTELLIGENCE AGENCY
DIRECTORATE OF INTELLIGENCE

22 December 1988
0930 EST

SPOT COMMENTARY: PAN AM 103: Analysis of Claims

We have received no forensic evidence to confirm the cause of the crash of Pan American Airlines Flight 103 yesterday; we do not rule out the possibility that a bomb was behind the crash.

Several groups have claimed responsibility for the incident in telephone calls in the United States and Europe:

--A male caller claimed that a group called the Guardians of the Islamic Revolution had destroyed the plane in retaliation for the US shootdown of an Iranian airliner last July.
--A caller claiming to represent the Islamic Jihad organization told ABC News in New York that the group had planted the bomb to commemorate Christmas.
--The Ulster Defense League allegedly issued a telephonic claim.
--Another anonymous caller claimed the plane had been downed by Mossad, the Israeli intelligence service.

We consider the claim from the Guardians of the Islamic Revolution as the most credible one received so far; previous attacks claimed by this group suggest it is pro-Iranian:

--Persons using this name have taken credit for the hijacking of an Air France flight from Frankfurt, West Germany in 1984; in that incident, an anonymous caller demanded that France release five persons imprisoned for attempting to kill former Iranian Prime Minister Bakhtiar in 1980. The group had taken credit for the assassination attempt as well.
--The Guardians of the Islamic Revolution claimed responsibility for an assassination attempt against a former Cabinet Minister of the Shah in London on 18 July 1987.
--In April 1988, the Guardians of Islam took credit for the bombing of a vehicle belonging to a German businessman employed with a firm involved in transfer of missile technology. The anonymous caller accused the businessman of providing missiles to Iraq, then at war with Iran.

An anonymous caller told a US diplomatic facility in Europe on 5 December that a bombing attempt would be made against a Pan American aircraft flying from Frankfurt, West Germany to the United States. The Federal Aviation Administration was notified of the threat and security for Pan Am flights out of Frankfurt was enhanced.

In the intervening years since Lockerbie there have been many claims and counter-claims about almost every aspect of the case. Conspiracy theories abound – some of them prompted by the presence of CIA officials on the plane. There has been endless discussion about whether or not the authorities had reacted properly to warnings of a terrorist attack apparently known to the intelligence services prior to Lockerbie. There have been repeated questions about the effectiveness of the security arrangements in Frankfurt, where the flight originated, and at Heathrow.

LINGERING DOUBTS

Most importantly of all from the point of view of the victims' families, serious doubts remain about the validity of al-Megrahi's conviction and the level of complicity of former Libyan leader Colonel Gaddafi in the crime. Although Libya paid compensation to Lockerbie victims, there has not been an unambiguous statement of responsibility by the Libyan government for the bombing of Pan Am Flight 103.

In the days and weeks that followed the disaster, the people of Lockerbie pulled together to deal with the tragedy. They helped to clear up debris from the crash and looked after the investigators, the relatives and the media who flooded into the town. There appears to be a strong sense that the community came together to deal with the tragedy and that this enabled the majority of people to get on with their lives. The 20th anniversary in 2008 was marked in a low-key way.

In a rather sombre twist to the story, the wreckage of the Pan Am jet still exists in a scrap-metal yard in

IN REMEMBRANCE OF ALL VICTIMS
OF LOCKERBIE AIR DISASTER
WHO DIED ON 21st DECEMBER 1988

STEVEN LEE BUTLER
1952 - 1988
"Life is life - Enjoy it"

Above: A wreath laying ceremony at the main memorial to the victims of the Lockerbie bombing at Dryfesdale Cemetery, just to the west of the town.

Lincolnshire. It was moved there after testing had been completed at Farnborough in Hampshire. The wreckage is being retained until the conclusion of all possible legal actions arising from the bombing.

SAD REMINDERS

In Lockerbie itself, there are numerous reminders of the events of 1988. New houses have been built in Sherwood Close, although a memorial garden stands on part of the area devastated by the explosion. The houses destroyed in Park Place have been rebuilt. The Dryfesdale Lodge Visitors Centre was opened in 2003. It is located in what had been a gravedigger's house at the cemetery. It includes exhibitions about the history of Lockerbie, including the bombing. It was built with

money from the local council and the Lockerbie Trust, which had been established after the bombing. The cemetery also houses the main memorial to the victims. There are books of remembrance in two local churches, a stained glass window in the town hall and a memorial room at Tundergarth, where the nose of the plane came down. There are also several memorials in the United States, because the majority of the victims from the plane were American.

One of the legacies of the events of December 1988 is the bond formed between the people of Lockerbie and the families of those who died in the plane – particularly the American families. Pan Am 103's victims included 35 people from Syracuse University in New York. There is a formal partnership between this university and the Lockerbie Academy. Two students from Lockerbie are given the opportunity to study at Syracuse each year.

MARDALE GREEN
FLOODED

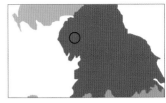

54° 31' 5" N, 2° 48' 24" W

18TH AUGUST, 1935

HAWESWATER, CUMBRIA, CA10 2RP

Above: The Dun Bull Hotel in Mardale in 1929. The hotel was a famous Lakeland inn, but it would be submerged with the rest of the village.

Above: Set among 800-year-old yew trees, the parish church was dismantled and the stone incorporated in the new dam.

VILLAGE SACRIFICED TO BUILD A RESERVOIR

There are scores of examples of lost settlements across Britain. Some have disappeared because of the impact of nature (for example, communities lost to the sea by erosion), but others, like Mardale Green in the Lake District, have been lost deliberately – sacrificed for an apparently greater public good.

Until the 1930s, Mardale Green was a small hamlet in the valley of Mardale in what was then Westmorland. Along with another small settlement, Measand, it lay next to Haweswater, then a natural lake. Both places

were farming communities. It was also a racing centre with the Mardale Hunt based nearby.

In the 1920s, however, Parliament gave the Manchester Corporation legal powers to create a reservoir in the valley to serve the growing need for water of its burgeoning population. The construction of the Haweswater Dam started in 1929, which required the abandonment of both Mardale Green and Measand. All the homes and farms in Mardale Green were demolished, along with the village pub. Most were blown up by the Royal Engineers. The remains of

Above: Seen from Mardale Ill Bell is the Small Water lake (foreground) and the southern end of Haweswater Reservoir in the distance.

almost a hundred people buried in the churchyard were exhumed and reburied at Shap.

There was an enormous local outcry at the time. The sacrificing of farming communities for the needs of urban communities miles away aroused strong passions. However, the opposition was in vain. The population of Mardale Green were moved elsewhere in the vicinity.

The final chapter in the story of the community of Mardale Green took place on Sunday, 18th August, 1935, when a farewell service was held in the village church of Holy Trinity. The service was an all-ticket affair with 75 people crammed into the small church. The Bishop of Carlisle offered a final blessing and the hymns included *O, God, Our Help in Ages Past*. Afterwards, the church was dismantled and the stone used in the building of the dam.

The valley was flooded and Haweswater Reservoir, with its capacity of more than 18 billion gallons, began supplying Manchester with water. With it the communities of the Mardale Valley disappeared forever – but not quite. When water levels are low in the reservoir, the remains of some buildings and a bridge can sometimes be seen.

CONISTON
WATER
TRAGEDY

54° 19' 14" N, 3° 5' 22" W

4TH JANUARY, 1967   CONISTON WATER, LAKE ROAD, CONISTON, CUMBRIA, LA21 8EW

DEATH OF DONALD CAMPBELL TRYING TO BREAK WORLD WATER SPEED RECORD

Above: Donald Campbell's jet-powered Bluebird at speed on Coniston Water on the fateful day of his accident, 4th January, 1967.

The tranquillity of Coniston Water more than 40 years on contrasts sharply with the moment of tragedy in 1967 when Donald Campbell died trying to break a world record on the lake. It was a dramatic event involving a man widely regarded as an archetypal British hero and it was captured fully on film. Therefore it is not surprising that the circumstances of Campbell's death have been discussed ever since.

LURE OF SPEED

Donald Campbell, like his father Malcolm Campbell, devoted his life to breaking speed records. He set seven world water speed records between 1955 and 1964, during which year he also held the world land speed record. He had arrived at Coniston in the autumn of 1966 with the aim of setting a new world water speed record of 300mph. Coniston was chosen because of its length and because it is straight.

His record attempt was made using his boat

Above: Donald Campbell in 1958. He appeared to be obsessed with emulating and surpassing his father's record breaking achievements.

Above: Donald Campbell with the sleek Bluebird K7 on Coniston Water in November 1966. He gained seven water speed records with the boat.

Bluebird K7, which had been fitted with a new engine. However, during November and December, Campbell was frustrated by technical problems with the boat and by bad weather. It was only after modifications had been made to *Bluebird* and better weather came along that Campbell was ready to make a serious attempt.

FATAL RUN

On Wednesday, 4th January, 1967, Campbell made a successful first run from north to south on Coniston, averaging 297mph. He turned and set off northwards but, on this second run, *Bluebird* left the water, rose into the air and then somersaulted and plunged back into the lake. Campbell's last words were recorded on the film of the record attempt as "I can't see anything in here; I've got the bows out; I'm going."

Campbell's body and the wreckage of *Bluebird* were finally recovered from Coniston between October 2000 and June 2001. Campbell was buried in Coniston Cemetery on 12th September, 2001.

There are three places in Coniston where Campbell and his achievements are recalled – a memorial opposite the car park in the centre of the village, at the cemetery in Hawkshead Old Road, where Campbell is buried, and also at the Bluebird Café at the lakeside. The Sun Inn, his base during the record attempt, is something of a Campbell shrine.

In addition, the Ruskin Museum has an extensive display about Donald Campbell, and the engine from *Bluebird* is kept there. A project is under way to restore and rebuild *Bluebird* and put it on display in the museum.

Above: Bluebird just moments before the fatal accident that took Campbell's life. The right-hand sponson has lifted clear of the water.

Above right: The stricken craft somersaults through the air before crashing back down into the lake and sinking with Campbell still aboard.

Below right: Bill Smith carries out the early stages of restoration on Bluebird K7 in a small North Shields workshop, on 7th December, 2005.

CARNFORTH STATION

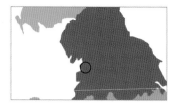

54° 7' 53" N, 2° 46' 16" W

EARLY 1945

WARTON ROAD, CARNFORTH, LANCASHIRE, LA5 9TR

WHERE 'BRIEF ENCOUNTER' WAS FILMED

The desire to see places where significant things happened is not confined to the locations of great events or tragedies. It extends to things that are the creation of fiction, of film and of television. Particularly in recent years, film and TV tourism has acquired a momentum of its own, with people keen to visit the locations where famous film or TV scenes were shot. Carnforth Station in Lancashire is among the most iconic of film locations in Britain because it was where *Brief Encounter* was filmed in the closing months of the Second World War.

Perhaps only in Britain could a film about a passionate, but unconsummated love affair be voted the most romantic film of all time. But the 1945 classic *Brief Encounter* achieved that distinction in a poll in 2010. Earlier, in 1999, it was voted the second best British film overall in a British Film Institute poll. For people of a certain age, *Brief Encounter* retains a charm and attraction, and the location where its famous station scenes were shot has become something of a place of pilgrimage.

A FINE ROMANCE

The film was written by Noël Coward, based on his earlier one-act stage play called *Still Life*. It was directed by one of the greatest directors in British film history, David Lean, and it starred Trevor Howard and Celia Johnson. It is the story of a chance encounter on a railway station platform between a woman played by Johnson in a comfortable, but boring marriage, and a dashing stranger, Howard. The film follows their

Above: An advertising poster for Brief Encounter, a very British love story. It earned Celia Johnson a nomination for an Academy Award.

Above: Scenes from the classic film Brief Encounter *with Celia Johnson and Trevor Howard, all based on the railway station at Carnforth.*

snatched relationship over a period of weeks before the stranger announces that he is leaving with his family to go to South Africa. As the cynics would say, nothing happens, but nevertheless, maybe because of that, it is still regarded as a classic.

PLATFORM SCENES

Much of the film was made in the studio at Denham in Buckinghamshire and in the nearby towns. However, the station scenes were filmed 200 miles away at Carnforth. It was chosen because it was considered to be away from danger areas for bombing and therefore blackout restrictions could be lifted. Filming was completed at night to avoid disrupting daytime train services. A considerable amount of action took place in the station's tearoom, the interior of which was recreated in the studio at Denham. The encounters on the platform and in the tunnels, and the distinctive clock, were all at Carnforth. Departure boards in the film quite clearly identify northern locations such as Leeds and Morecambe.

Carnforth Station had been a busy junction on the West Coast mainline at the time of the making of the film. However, the rail service in the area was a victim of the Beeching cuts of the 1960s. In 1970 the mainline platforms were removed, but the station still has services running to many parts of the North of England.

Many of the buildings fell into disrepair and the station had a rundown air for many years. However, due to its starring role in such an enduring film, renovation took place, and in 2003 a heritage centre and a restored Brief Encounter café were opened. The heritage centre features exhibitions that recall Carnforth's war years.

Above: Margaret Barton, who took the part of the tea-room assistant in the film, recreates her role in the refurbished café at the station.

Above: The refurbished Carnforth station and its historic clock, which featured prominently in the film Brief Encounter.

BLACKPOOL
OPEN-AIR BATHS

53° 47' 39" N, 3° 3' 26" W

1923–1981   SANDCASTLE WATERPARK, SOUTH BEACH, BLACKPOOL, LANCASHIRE, FY4 1BB

AT ONE TIME THE LARGEST OUTDOOR SWIMMING BATHS IN THE WORLD

Above: Taking the plunge. A swimmer dives from the top of the diving platform into the crowded water of the pool below.

Above: Blackpool's massive outdoor swimming pool seen from the air in 1955. Its buildings displayed classically-styled architecture.

Above: After the open-air bath was demolished in the 1980s, the Sandcastle waterpark was constructed on the site.

Above: Wish you were here? Souvenir postcards show Blackpool's open-air baths in their heyday, when crowds would flock to take a dip.

If ever anything symbolised seaside leisure in Britain between the two world wars, it was the open-air swimming bath or lido. They were the craze during the 1920s and 1930s, and seaside towns up and down the country rushed to build them as symbols of municipal pride.

Blackpool, which regarded itself then, and still does, as the leading seaside resort in the country, was not to be beaten when it came to open-air swimming baths. In 1923 it opened a gigantic one in classical style, with proportions to match, on the South Beach. £75,000 (around £3.5m at 2012 prices) was spent to create a pool that was wider than an Olympic pool was long, measuring 116 metres long by 53 metres wide. It was designed to stage events as well as entertain holidaymakers. It had a diving area and a championship pool. The pool could accommodate 1,500 bathers and 8,000 spectators, and there were changing facilities for 600. At the time of its opening, bathers paid the equivalent of about £1.25 at 2012 prices for a swim.

KNOCKOUT FUN

For many years before and after the Second World War, the baths flourished. They were the scene of bathing competitions and a host of other events, including the wacky 1970s and 1980s TV series *It's A Knockout*. The demise of the Blackpool open-air baths was a metaphor for the challenges facing resorts like Blackpool. The affordability of foreign holidays with almost guaranteed sunshine drew people away from the traditional resorts like Blackpool, which were forced to reinvent themselves to tackle the vicissitudes of the British weather.

So, in 1983, demolition of the baths, which had been shut since 1981, was started. An indoor waterpark, the Sandcastle, was opened in June 1986 by a public/private-sector partnership on the site.

PRESTON
BY-PASS

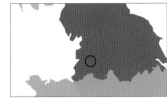

53° 45' 54" N, 2° 38' 23" W

BRITAIN'S FIRST STRETCH OF MOTORWAY

Above: At a stately pace, Prime Minister Harold Macmillan's car leads the first car along Britain's first section of motorway, the Preston By-Pass.

The idea of establishing motorways in Britain first took hold in the 1930s, when other countries, notably Germany, Italy and the United States, started doing so. As early as 1936 the Institution of Highway Engineers published a plan for 3,000 miles of motorway in Britain, but it was only after the Second World War that plans were properly developed.

Lancashire was at the forefront of the motorway revolution, largely because of the foresight and determination of one man – Sir James Drake. Drake had visited the German autobahns in the thirties and this had convinced him that motorways were vital to improve journey times, to reduce congestion and to increase safety on the roads.

Drake, who worked for Blackpool Borough Council before the war, joined Lancashire County Council in 1945. Despite the austerity of post-war Britain, he pushed the case for motorways and in 1949 he produced a Road Plan for Lancashire, which envisaged, among other routes, a major north-south motorway through the county. Drake pressed the Government and eventually approval was given to build a first section of motorway as a by-pass for Preston and as a 'guinea pig' for motorway development across the country. A corridor of land had been protected for a number of years to allow construction.

The Preston By-Pass was built by Tarmac Construction and the 8¼-mile section of road was opened by the Prime Minister, Harold Macmillan, on 5th December, 1958. Originally, Drake and his colleagues had argued for a three-lane highway, but the Ministry of Transport only allowed two lanes, and at first there was no hard shoulder and no speed limit. Perhaps astonishingly, given the vociferous opposition to some road building schemes in later years, there were very few objections to the proposal and no public inquiry was held.

The film of the opening shows the Prime Minister's convoy proceeding gracefully along the pristine new carriageway. Within a month of the opening, the engineers who had built it had an embarrassment on their hands. They were forced to close the road and divert the traffic onto the old roads because the motorway surface had been damaged by severe frost. Many lessons were learnt about how to deal with surface water on new motorways. The next section of what became the M6 was the Lancaster By-Pass, opened in 1960, and then further sections were added as the motorway network developed in the following years.

On 5th December, 2008, on the 50th anniversary of the opening of the Preston By-Pass, the 'missing link' of the M6, connecting its northerly end with the A74(M) across the Scottish Border, was opened. On the same day, a plaque commemorating the achievements of Sir James Drake, who had died in 1989, was unveiled near Junction 31 of the M6 alongside the original Preston section of the motorway. By 2012 there were more than 2,000 miles of motorway across Britain.

Above: Prime Minister Harold Macmillan (L) and Transport Minister Harold Watkinson (C) marvel at the wonders of the Preston By-Pass.

Above: This view of the Preston By-Pass shows it still under construction in August 1958. It was the beginning of a new era in road building.

Above: The blue plaque commemorating the achievements of Sir James Drake set on a plinth alongside the Preston section of the M6.

Above: In contrast to the traffic volumes of the late 1950s when the first motorway section was opened, today the M6 is constantly crowded.

PEEL PARK
ACCRINGTON

10TH MARCH, 1962   PEEL PARK, ALICE STREET, ACCRINGTON, LANCASHIRE, BB5 6QR

HOME OF THE FIRST CLUB TO GO OUT OF THE FOOTBALL LEAGUE MID-SEASON

Above: The overgrown and derelict Peel Park ground in June 1969, once the home of proud football team Accrington Stanley.

The name Accrington Stanley still conjures up misty-eyed romanticism among older football fans. In 1962 the club became the first to leave the Football League mid-season for financial reasons, but many supporters and local people still believe they were forced out unnecessarily.

In the 21st century, football clubs move between the Football League and the lower leagues in an organised 'pyramid' system of promotion and relegation. Back in 1962 things were different. It was quite something when a club went out of the League – even more so when it happened during the season and in controversial circumstances.

During the 1961/62 season, Accrington Stanley's performance both on and off the pitch was poor. The financial position came to a head in early 1962, when the club's debts were revealed to be at least £60,000 (around £1m at 2012 values). An attempt to save the club, including a public appeal, was unsuccessful.

RESCUE ATTEMPT

Many fans believed that the purchase of an old stand from the Aldershot Military Tattoo Ground four years earlier was the beginning of the slide. Others were deeply suspicious of the role of Bob Lord, chairman of neighbouring Burnley Football Club, who was involved in the rescue attempt, but who many thought was keen to see the end of a rival local club.

Accrington Stanley's last game was a 4–0 defeat at Crewe on 2nd March. The scheduled home game against Exeter City on 10th March never took place. The League accepted their letter of resignation and the club dropped out of the Fourth Division.

FALL TO DERELICTION

The club struggled on in the Lancashire Combination but went out of business with huge debts in 1966. Peel Park was taken over by the local council and lay derelict for some years before finally being demolished in the late 1970s. There is virtually no trace of the old Peel Park ground left, although one structure – originally a supporters' club building – still stands. The area is now a playing field for the adjacent Peel Park Primary School.

However, the name Accrington Stanley lives on and is back in the Football League. In 1968, two years after the original 'Stanley' folded, a new club was formed, which now plays at the Crown Ground elsewhere in the town. The club rose through the ranks of non-League football and, in 2006, league football returned to Accrington when 'Stanley' were promoted back into the Football League as champions of the Football Conference.

Above: The main stand at the Peel Park ground looks out over a forlorn pitch strewn with debris from years of neglect.

Above: Once the vantage point of dedicated 'Stanley' fans, the decrepit main stand crumbles as it awaits demolition.

HAÇIENDA
MANCHESTER

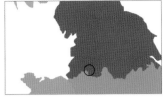

53° 28' 32" N, 2° 14' 15" W

1982–1997   HAÇIENDA APARTMENTS, WHITWORTH STREET, MANCHESTER, M1 5DD

BRIEFLY THE MOST FAMOUS NIGHTCLUB IN THE WORLD

Above: The old warehouse building on Whitworth Street in Manchester that was home to the Haçienda Club.

Like many places featured on this journey, The Haçienda is a place that captured a specific phenomenon in a particular place at a particular time. Also like many places on this journey, it has probably acquired an even greater reputation and celebrity since its demise. However, The Haçienda was a focal point for the music scene of the 1980s and 1990s, when Manchester, or 'Madchester' as it became known, was at the heart of things.

The Haçienda opened in 1982 in a building at 11–13 Whitworth Street in Manchester city centre. The building was originally a warehouse, later a yacht builder's yard and then in the 1970s a Bollywood Cinema. The money to create the club came from Factory Records and the band New Order. One of the prime movers was Tony Wilson, the Factory label boss and Granada TV presenter.

The club, which was designed by Ben Kelly, made the most of the industrial fabric of the building. It consisted of a dance area and bar upstairs, and a series of bars downstairs, named quixotically after Anthony Blunt, Kim Philby and other Britons who spied for the Soviet Union in the 1950s.

Some of the most famous names of the music scene

Above: Associated with the rise of acid house and rave music, The Haçienda had an 'industrial' interior designed by Ben Kelly.

of the late 20th century played The Haçienda, including The Smiths, Madonna and Curtis Mayfield. However, the DJs who worked there also became well known, including Dave Haslam, Jon Da Silva, Mike Pickering and Graeme Park.

GOLDEN PERIOD

The nightclub never really made any money and was consistently supported financially over the years by New Order and Factory Records. During the first few years the club was primarily a live music venue. Its golden period was the late 1980s, when the crowds started to flock and The Haçienda was the leading club in the country. It was one of the first clubs to play house music and its Friday 'Nude Nights' were legendary.

However, the late 1980s saw the beginning of problems that eventually brought down The Haçienda. In July 1989, 16-year-old Claire Leighton took ecstasy in the club and later died. There was frequently violence on the premises and the police wanted to close it down.

The final gig was on 28th June, 1997. The Haçienda was used as an art gallery for a period and for some one-off music events. In 2000, the fixtures and fittings were snapped up at an auction and in 2002 the club was demolished. Luxury apartments were built on the site.

A film by Michael Winterbottom, *24 Hour Party People*, starring Steve Coogan, was made in 2001 in a reconstituted replica of the club in East Manchester.

Above: Peter Hook (L) of the band New Order and Tony Wilson, prime movers behind The Haçienda, look on as the demolition men move in.

Above: A ticket stub for a gig by New Order at The Haçienda. The band's record sales helped to keep the club afloat.

HAROLD SHIPMAN'S
SURGERY

53° 27' 8" N, 2° 4' 50" W

7TH SEPTEMBER, 1998

21 MARKET STREET, HYDE, GREATER MANCHESTER, SK14 2AD

THE PLACE WHERE BRITAIN'S MOST PROLIFIC SERIAL KILLER PRACTISED

Far left: The unassuming exterior of Dr Shipman's surgery in Hyde, where at least six of his victims are thought to have died.

Left: Harold Shipman 18 months before he was arrested. Who would know that they were looking at the face of a mass murderer?

As with so many locations where momentous and terrible events have taken place, there's nothing now to indicate what happened at 21 Market Street in Hyde. In 2012, more than a decade after Dr Harold Shipman was convicted of murdering 15 of his patients, the building where he practised as a GP was empty. It sits unobtrusively among the other shops in the busy shopping area of Hyde, on the eastern side of Greater Manchester. Unless you knew, you would have no reason to know that this was the base for a man who is generally considered to have murdered more than 200 of his patients, making him Britain's most prolific mass murderer.

LETHAL DOSES

Shipman's *modus operandi* was to befriend his elderly female patients and then administer lethal doses of diamorphine. He forged their medical records to suggest that they had been in poor health and then signed their death certificates. It is believed that at least six of his victims died in his surgery, although most of the lethal doses were administered on home visits.

Shipman first came to the attention of the police in 1998, when fellow doctors became concerned about the high number of cremation certificates for elderly women being signed by Shipman. After an initial investigation, police concluded there was insufficient evidence. However, Shipman's downfall came after he forged the will of his last victim, Kathleen Grundy. There were suspicions about the authenticity of her will because it excluded her family and gave money to Shipman. Her body was exhumed and traces of diamorphine were discovered. Shipman was arrested on 7th September, 1998.

KILLER'S DEMISE

On 31st January, 2000, Shipman was found guilty of the murders and of forgery of a will, and sentenced to life with a recommendation that he never be released. Home Secretary David Blunkett ordered a whole-life tariff for Shipman. In January 2004 Shipman hanged himself in his cell at Wakefield Prison.

The official inquiry headed by Dame Janet Smith concluded that Shipman's killing had started much earlier in his career and included victims from his time in Pontefract and Todmorden in West Yorkshire as well as his practices in Hyde.

After Shipman's arrest, the practice in Market Street was run directly by the local health authority, using locum GPs. Many of Shipman's former patients returned there to see new doctors who took over the practice. The surgery was redecorated and brightened up. Later it was taken over by a new medical practice until 2004, when they moved to a new location. The premises were later used as an electrical store, but in early 2012 were empty.

Families of the victims of Harold Shipman have established a memorial to their loved ones, called the Garden of Tranquility, which opened in Hyde Park in Hyde in July 2005.

The Shipman case led to significant changes in medical practice, including the procedures for certifying deaths, for the monitoring of doctors, the running of the General Medical Council and the handling of drugs by doctors.

Above: Dr Harold Shipman's surgery at the Market Street practice in Hyde, as it was in 2000 at the time of his conviction.

NATIONAL CENTRE FOR POPULAR MUSIC

53° 22' 39" N, 1° 27' 55" W

1999–2000   SHEFFIELD HALLAM UNIVERSITY STUDENTS UNION, PATERNOSTER ROW, SHEFFIELD, S1 2QQ

Above: The striking stainless steel-clad architecture of the National Centre for Popular Music wowed visitors when it opened on 1st March, 1999.

The story of the National Centre for Popular Music is a story of great enthusiasm, of grand projects in a time of relative plenty and of a dramatic crashing to earth almost as soon as it had begun. The National Lottery started in Britain in 1994 and in the run-up to the millennium a number of major projects were started, largely funded by the lottery, all intended as contributions to the millennium celebrations. Others included a number of science centres around the country and the National Space Centre in Leicester.

DRUM ROLL

The idea of a national centre to celebrate the heritage of popular music in Britain sounded like a winner. It was the brainchild of Tim Strickland, who had previously been associated with the band The Specials, and who was working for Sheffield City Council at the time. It was hoped that the centre would bring large numbers of visitors into an area of Sheffield that was being developed into a cultural quarter.

The building, which cost £16m, had a distinctive appearance. It consisted of four giant stainless steel drums surrounding an atrium. One of the drums housed a 3D surround-sound auditorium called Soundscapes; two others were Making Music and Perspectives, and the fourth was intended as an area for touring exhibitions.

DISCORDANT NOTE

The centre opened on 1st March, 1999 and its business plan was based on a target of 400,000 visitors a year. This proved to be wildly optimistic. In the first seven months, by October of 1999, just over 100,000 people had visited. PricewaterhouseCoopers were brought in. The original chief executive left and visitor number targets were revised downwards.

Most commentators agreed that the problem was the content. It was highly interactive and offered plenty of opportunities for visitors to get a taste of music making. However, it didn't contain much rock and pop memorabilia and that was what people expected.

Despite a relaunch in early 2000 and the resignation of a second chief executive, the centre closed in June 2000. The building was briefly used as a music venue, then taken over by the regional development agency, Yorkshire Forward, which sold it to Sheffield Hallam University in 2003 for use by the student union.

A MILLENNIUM-FUNDED VENTURE THAT NEVER TOOK OFF

Above: Russell Dawson from Sheffield plays air guitar during a visit to the National Centre for Popular Music on the day that it opened.

Above: Young Sarah Rayner strikes a rock chick pose in front of a video wall at the centre. It contained many interactive displays.

HILLSBOROUGH
DISASTER

53° 23' 55" N, 1° 29' 18" W

15TH APRIL, 1989   HILLSBOROUGH FOOTBALL GROUND, PENISTONE ROAD, SHEFFIELD, S6 1SW

SCENE OF BRITAIN'S WORST FOOTBALL STADIUM DISASTER

Above: To escape the crush in the lower tier of the Leppings Lane Stand, fans are hauled up to the upper tier.

Above: Shocked fans leave the Hillsborough ground after the tragedy. It led to widespread safety improvements to stadia throughout the country.

There are many examples of places where great tragedies occur that are torn down or redeveloped, often as a way of exorcising the memories of what happened there. However, the Leppings Lane Stand at Hillsborough football ground, where Britain's worst football stadium disaster occurred in 1989, is still there and it still houses supporters week in and week out.

The events of the afternoon of Saturday, 15th April, 1989 are still hauntingly familiar. Hillsborough was a tragedy that unfolded in front of a television audience. The occasion was the FA Cup Semi-Final between Liverpool and Nottingham Forest being played, as FA Cup semi-finals often were, at Hillsborough, one of the Football Association's favoured neutral venues for such matches.

At the time the Leppings Lane upper tier was seated, but the lower tier comprised standing terraces divided into a series of pens. In common with all major football grounds at the time, there were high perimeter fences around the pitch to stop fans from invading the playing area. The building of these fences had been a direct response to the hooliganism that blighted football during the 1970s and 1980s.

FANS SURGE IN

Liverpool's supporters were being accommodated in the Leppings Lane end of the ground, but as the kick-off approached at three o'clock many fans were still outside the ground. To prevent a crush, the police opened gates normally used as exits from the ground to allow fans into the standing areas in the lower tier of the Leppings Lane stand. Instead of spreading out into all the pens, the fans poured into the central ones because there was no one controlling the crowd. A crush soon developed, with supporters near the front of the pen forced up against the perimeter fencing and unable to escape. It was later estimated that there were around 3,000 people in the pen, whereas there should have been only 1,600.

The game was stopped after six minutes, once it became clear that a problem of major proportions was unfolding. Some fans escaped the crush by being hauled up onto the upper tier. Others tried to break the fence down and climb onto the pitch.

The final death toll was 96 people, ranging in ages from 10 to 67, including one fan, Tony Bland, who remained in a persistent vegetative state for almost four years until his life support machines were switched off in March 1993.

The widespread shock felt across the football world and the country led to the postponement of many matches. There was even talk of the FA Cup being abandoned for the season. However, the match was replayed at Old Trafford on 7th May, when Liverpool won 3–1 before going on to beat Merseyside rivals Everton 3–2 in the final.

POLICE CRITICISED

The police were criticised for their handling of the build-up of fans before the crush and for their response once injured fans began spilling onto the pitch. There were also allegations that there had been crushing at the ground before, but that nothing had been done to deal

Below: Chaos reigns as injured fans are laid out on the pitch and others realise how lucky they are to have escaped the crush.

Above: Advertising boards are broken up and used as makeshift stretchers to carry away the victims of the crush.

with it. The official inquiry into the disaster, headed by Lord Justice Taylor, concluded that the primary reason for the tragedy was the failure of police control. His main recommendations had far-reaching consequences for football – mainly the removal of perimeter fences and the introduction of all-seater stadia for games in the top divisions.

The inquest into the deaths recorded verdicts of accidental death, which angered the relatives of the victims. A private prosecution of two police officers collapsed when one was ruled unfit to stand trial. Legal cases continued well into the new century, and in 2011 previously secret papers relating to the case were released.

As the legal arguments continued to rage, Hillsborough went back to its regular life as a football ground. The Leppings Lane stand was shut for two years and reopened in 1991 with the lower tier converted into an all-seater stand – a direct consequence of the report that arose from the disaster that happened there. Hillsborough's South Stand was completely revamped for the Euro 96 tournament. Overall, though, Hillsborough remains very much as it was at the time of the tragedy.

There are several memorials to the victims of the disaster in and around Liverpool. At Hillsborough itself, the official memorial to those who died is near the main entrance of the stadium in Parkside Road. There's also another memorial outside the ground near the Leppings Lane end. A short service is held each year near the memorial in Sheffield to remember the victims.

TRAGIC IMPACT

The impact on Hillsborough itself though was a strangely muted one. Although the disaster happened in Sheffield, the victims were nearly all associated with Liverpool and most of the scenes of grief that were played out very publicly in the weeks and months following the tragedy happened there. Even more than 20 years later, the anger felt by the families of those who died and by the wider community on Merseyside is still strong.

Hillsborough remains one of the most seismic events in the sporting history of Britain, coming as it did only a few years after two other major stadium disasters – the fire at Bradford City and the crush at the European Cup Final (where Liverpool were playing) in Belgium. As well as the impact on those directly involved, it changed the face of football forever, transforming the character of stadia in Britain and beyond.

BATTLE OF
ORGREAVE

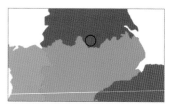

53° 22' 41" N, 1° 21' 54" W

18TH JUNE, 1984   WAVERLEY DEVELOPMENT, ORGREAVE, NEAR ROTHERHAM, SOUTH YORKSHIRE.

SCENE OF THE 'BATTLE OF ORGREAVE' DURING THE MINERS' STRIKE

Above: In one of numerous incidents during the miners' strike, before the most violent battle on 18th June, police deliver a concerted push against a section of the miners' picket line outside the Orgreave Coking Plant, on 1st June, 1984.

If ever there was an example of how a place name, previously largely unknown to people outside the immediate area, has become a byword for something, then it is Orgreave. If ever there was an example of a place thrust into the national consciousness through a single event on a single day, out of an almost random set of circumstances, then it is Orgreave. It was on Monday, 18th June, 1984 that one of the most violent clashes in British industrial history took place in a small village near Rotherham in South Yorkshire.

The 'Battle of Orgreave' took place during the miners' strike, which ran from March 1984 to March 1985. The industrial action by the National Union of Mineworkers, led by Arthur Scargill, was in protest at plans by the National Coal Board, led by Sir Ian Macgregor, to close coalmines across Britain, drastically reducing the number of mining jobs.

MINERS PRE-EMPTED

The dispute was one of the most bitter in post-war Britain and it ended eventually with the miners' defeat – partly because the Government had made sure that the impact of the strike was minimised by stockpiling supplies of coal at power stations before it started.

There were many violent clashes between striking miners and the police during the strike, but the events of 18th June in South Yorkshire are probably remembered as the most dramatic flashpoint of the dispute.

Orgreave produced coke from coal for use in steel furnaces. The NUM organised a picket to try to prevent lorries leaving the plant. The police were said to have been aware of the NUM plans in advance, it was later claimed, through MI5 infiltration and the phone tapping of miners' leaders. An estimated 5,000–6,000 miners faced a larger number of police in a field near the plant.

VIOLENT CONFRONTATION

In a confrontation that lasted several hours, there were repeated clashes as the miners surged forward and as the police, including around 50 mounted officers, charged the pickets. At one point Arthur Scargill stepped out in front of the picket line and was seen on TV being manhandled by police. There was also hand-to-hand fighting between police and pickets. According to official reports, there were 91 arrests that day. Fifty-one pickets and 72 police officers were injured. Almost 100 pickets were charged, but the trials of those whose cases eventually came to court collapsed.

Plans to scale down the number of pits continued after 1984, and by 2012 there were only a handful of deep mines remaining in Britain compared with 174 in 1983. The remaining mining in Britain is now all privately run.

After the strike, the Orgreave Coking Plant continued in operation until 1990. The area was used for opencast mining until 2006, when extraction ceased. Since then the whole area is being redeveloped under the new name of Waverley.

Plans have been approved for the building of almost 4,000 new homes and the first houses were being built in early 2012. There are also plans for offices and industrial units, but parts of Orgreave will be retained as open land, including the area where the confrontation took place back in 1984.

Left: A badge depicting a miner being charged by a baton-wielding mounted policeman commemorates the pitched battle on 18th June, 1984.

Below: Miners' leader Arthur Scargill (C) during a march by trade unionists through Central London in support of the miners, with Labour MP Tony Benn (second R), on 27th June, 1984.

HARROGATE'S
OLD SWAN
HOTEL

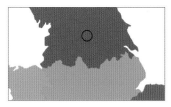

53° 59' 45" N, 1° 32' 50" W

14TH DECEMBER, 1926   OLD SWAN HOTEL, SWAN ROAD, HARROGATE, NORTH YORKSHIRE, HG1 2SR

THE SCENE OF AGATHA CHRISTIE'S
MYSTERIOUS DISAPPEARANCE

Above: The Old Swan Hotel, Harrogate, pictured in 2012, scene of author Agatha Christie's mysterious disappearance in 1926.

It was at what is now the Old Swan Hotel in Harrogate that the mystery of a celebrity disappearance, sparking a massive police operation across the country, came to an end just before Christmas in 1926. Agatha Christie, who was already established as a successful crime writer, had disappeared from her home in Sunningdale in Berkshire on 3rd December. Her car was found abandoned off the road at Newlands Corner, near Guildford in Surrey. The only clue to her disappearance was a letter she left for her secretary saying she was going to Yorkshire.

For 11 days more than a thousand police were involved in the search for her, but her whereabouts remained elusive. In fact, Christie had boarded a train to Harrogate and had checked in at the Swan Hydropathic Hotel in the spa town. For more than a week she apparently mingled with fellow guests, enjoying the food and entertainment, without being spotted. This was despite the massive publicity surrounding her disappearance. However, she was eventually recognised by a banjo player at the hotel called Bob Tappin and the police were alerted. Christie's husband, Archibald, arrived at the hotel on 14th December to collect her.

PUBLIC REACTION

Christie never spoke about the missing 11 days of her life. Nor did she ever reveal the real reason for her disappearance. Some people dismissed it as an elaborate publicity stunt. Most believe that it was connected with the unhappiness in her marriage to Archibald, which was to end in divorce two years later. It is known that the couple had quarrelled on the night of her disappearance, after Archibald revealed that he was in love with another woman, Nancy Neele, and wanted a divorce.

Christie checked in at the hotel in the name of Teresa Neele and many people believe the disappearance was designed to embarrass her husband. Public reaction at the time was not very sympathetic to Christie. Some people thought she wanted to convince the police that her husband had killed her.

At the time, her husband claimed she had suffered memory loss brought on by the apparent car crash. One of her biographers believes that she was suffering from a rare condition known as 'fugue state' – a form of amnesia brought on by the stress of her unhappy marriage and the recent death of her mother.

Christie, who remarried after her divorce from Archibald, continued her career as a hugely successful novelist. Her most famous characters were Hercule Poirot and Miss Marple, and in total she wrote 66 novels and 14 short-story collections, as well as writing under a pseudonym. More than four billion copies of her novels have been sold worldwide and it is claimed that she is the best-selling author of all time. She died in 1976.

The hotel that was the scene of her mysterious disappearance changed its name in the mid-1950s to the Old Swan Hotel, as Harrogate sought to move away from its traditional spa image and adapt for a new age. The 1979 film *Agatha* starring Dustin Hoffman and Vanessa Redgrave, which featured the story of her disappearance, was partly filmed at the hotel.

The Wedgwood Restaurant where Christie dined during the 11 days of her disappearance is still in use. The room where she is believed to have stayed was on the ground floor, but it no longer exists. However, one of the hotel's executive suites, Room 253, is named after her. Partly on the back of its Agatha Christie connection, Harrogate started a crime writing festival in 2003, which uses the Old Swan as a base.

Left: Agatha Christie, pictured in 1950, long after the mystery of her disappearance that could have come straight from the pages of one of her own novels.

Right: The front page story in the Daily Mirror, 7th December, 1926, after Christie had been missing for four days, sparking a massive police operation.

AVRO AIRCRAFT FACTORY
LEEDS

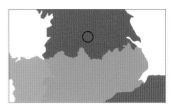

53° 52' 25" N, 1° 39' 48" W

1939–1946   LEEDS-BRADFORD AIRPORT INDUSTRIAL ESTATE, YEADON, LEEDS, WEST YORKSHIRE, LS19 7WP

A HIDDEN AEROPLANE FACTORY DURING THE SECOND WORLD WAR

Above: Avro's sprawling aircraft production factory was disguised with grass covering the roof so that it could not be spotted by enemy aircraft flying overhead.

Above: The factory, pictured in 2012, is a modified version of the original building from the 1940s.

Today it is an anonymous looking industrial estate alongside Leeds-Bradford Airport. Between 1939 and 1946 it was an industrial production centre contributing to the war effort on a gargantuan scale.

Leeds and Bradford Municipal Aerodrome had opened in October 1931 and regular flights linking it with London and Newcastle were established. When war broke out in 1939, Avro built what was called a 'shadow factory' alongside the aerodrome to contribute to the aircraft production needed for the war effort.

ELABORATE DISGUISE

The factory, which covered a million-and-a-half square feet in area, was said to be the largest single factory unit in Europe. It was one of a number of shadow factories built around the country for wartime aircraft production. Its size and its significance meant that it was considered to be at high risk of being a target for enemy bombers.

An elaborate camouflaging operation took place, masterminded by people who had previously worked in the film industry. The camouflage consisted of grass covering the roof of the factory, replicating the original field pattern, with imitation farm buildings, stone walls and a duck pond in the area around the factory. Hedges and bushes made out of fabric were changed to match the changing colours of the seasons and dummy animals were moved around daily to increase the camouflage. It worked because the factory was never detected by enemy bombers and remained untouched throughout the war.

MASSIVE WORKFORCE

At the height of its operation, more than 17,500 people, mostly conscripts, worked there. The factory was an assembly plant that was in production 24 hours a day. Workers, who were bussed in from all over West Yorkshire, worked 69 hours a week on a three days, followed by three nights basis. Extra homes were built in the surrounding towns to accommodate such a large workforce.

Gracie Fields was among the well-known wartime entertainers who visited the factory to entertain the workers. More than 5,000 at a time crammed into the works canteen for concerts.

PRODUCTION LINE

Throughout the course of the war, Avro Yeadon produced almost 700 Lancaster bombers, 4,500 Ansons and several other types of aircraft. A taxiway was built from the factory to the aerodrome, which was extended so that it could become a test centre for military flights.

The airfield resumed civilian flights in 1947 and subsequently developed into Leeds-Bradford International Airport. The Avro factory was closed in 1946, but the site is now the Leeds-Bradford Airport Industrial Estate. The estate's main building is the same one, albeit modified and without the camouflage, that housed the aircraft factory during the war. The remains of the taxiway from the factory to the main airfield are still visible.

There was also a Royal Ordnance Corps site opposite the Avro factory and some remains of that can be seen in what is now a secure parking area and caravan park. A plaque commemorating the role of Avro Yeadon is displayed inside the airport's terminal building. It is still remarkable to imagine, as you drive along the A658 past the industrial estate, that this was once a secret factory that contributed so much to Britain's war effort.

Above: Row upon row of Lancaster bombers and other aircraft were contained within the vast factory. Almost 700 of the heavy bombers were built during the course of the Second World War.

Above: More then 17,000 workers were employed at the Avro Yeadon assembly plant, which was in production 24 hours a day to keep up with the demands of the war effort.

HARRY RAMSDEN'S
LEEDS

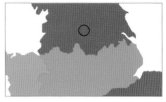

53° 52' 39" N, 1° 43' 30" W

1928–2011

WHITE CROSS, GUISELEY, LEEDS, WEST YORKSHIRE, LS20 8LZ

THE SITE OF THE FIRST HARRY RAMSDEN'S FISH-AND-CHIP SHOP

Above: The original hut, from which the enterprising Harry Ramsden Jnr first sold his popular takeaway fish-and-chips in 1928 was preserved for many years by the owners of the main Guiseley restaurant that stood alongside.

Fish-and-chips enjoy an iconic place in British culinary history, and Harry Ramsden's establishment occupies a special place in that story. It was a story that began in a small hut in Guiseley near Leeds in 1928.

Harry Ramsden's father (also called Harry) had started selling fish-and-chips in Bradford before the First World War. Harry Jnr, who had previously been a mill worker and a publican, bought a small hut for £150 and opened a takeaway fish-and-chip shop next to a tram stop in Guiseley, midway between Leeds, Bradford and Ilkley.

His fish and chips proved highly popular and three years later he built a sit-down restaurant, which opened on 20th December, 1931. It is said that he modelled the interior on the Ritz Hotel in London. Ramsden's idea was to bring an air of elegance to the eating of the great British working-class staple. So the new restaurant featured stained-glass windows, chandeliers and tablecloths.

FAME AND FORTUNE

The fame of Harry Ramsden's at Guiseley quickly spread and people flocked from all over Yorkshire and beyond for the experience. The restaurant was expanded and could accommodate 275 diners. It was reckoned to be the largest fish-and-chip restaurant in the world.

In 1954, Harry Ramsden sold the restaurant to his long-term business partner, Eddie Stokes, and the business was subsequently sold on several times. The reputation of the restaurant grew. It was popular with celebrities including Russell Harty and Jimmy Saville. Margaret Thatcher saw the political advantages of allying herself with a popular northern brand and visited during the 1983 and 1987 General Election campaigns. Harry Corbett, the creator of Sooty and the nephew of Harry Ramsden, occasionally played the piano there to entertain guests.

For almost the first 60 years of its life, the Harry Ramsden's business was just a single restaurant in Guiseley. However, after 1988, when it was bought by Merryweather's and subsequently sold on to Granada, it expanded with other restaurants opening elsewhere in Britain and even overseas. The brand was also extended into motorway service stations. In the early 2000s, there were further ownership changes and in 2010 it was bought by Boparan Ventures Limited (BVL).

In 2011, the fortunes of the brand overall were still healthy, but according to the company, the original Harry Ramsden's was losing money. In November, BVL announced the planned closure of the Guiseley home of Harry Ramsden's. It shut its doors on 19th December, 2011 – exactly 80 years bar one day after it had opened.

The closure provoked local opposition and a wave of nostalgia for the heritage of Harry Ramsden's. However, the restaurant was taken over and reopened by the Wetherby Whaler chain in 2012 and many of the distinctive Ramsden's features were retained, including the stained-glass windows and the ornate plasterwork.

Above: With the success of the original takeway fish-and-chip shop, Harry Ramsden expanded into larger premises with fitted carpets, oak-panelled walls and chandeliers – the roof topped by a distinctive clock.

Above: The elegant interior of Ramsden's original Guiseley restaurant could accommodate 275 diners, who were entertained with lived music while they ate. The restaurant served almost a million customers a year.

JOWETT CAR FACTORY
BRADFORD

53° 49' 45" N, 1° 43' 56" W

1919–1954

BRADFORD ROAD, IDLE, BRADFORD, WEST YORKSHIRE, BD10 8EG

THE RETAIL PARK WHERE MUCH-LOVED CARS WERE ONCE MADE

Above: The Jowett car factory in Idle, near Bradford, was built on the site of a disused quarry, and car making started there in 1920 with the Jowett Seven light car.

A retail park on the outskirts of Bradford encapsulates one aspect of the change in the British economy in the second half of the 20th century. Like many other sites all over Britain, a place where things were made is now a place where things are sold. The site of a former car factory has become a retail park. Of course, as many economists will tell you, we still make things and there is a view that it doesn't matter whether we make things as long as we can sell things. Nevertheless, there's a romance associated with the manufacturing industry, particularly when the product involved has achieved a cult following. One such product is the Jowett car in its various models.

Jowett had begun as a company elsewhere in Bradford in 1901, founded by the brothers Benjamin and William

Jowett. They were among the early pioneers of car manufacturing in Britain, with their emphasis being on the production of light, affordable cars.

COLLECTORS' ITEMS

The company moved to the Springfield Works site in Idle in 1919 and, for the next 35 years, it produced cars and vans there, including many that have become collectors' items since. Many models of cars and vans were made at the factory. Among them, the Kestrel, the Ken, the Jupiter and the Javelin still evoke fond memories among car enthusiasts.

After the Second World War the company was sold, but by the mid-1950s it was in financial difficulties. Jowett stopped making cars at the Idle factory in 1954, but continued in business for a while, making aircraft parts and spare parts for Jowett vehicles, at a site elsewhere in Yorkshire. However, the Idle site was sold to International Harvester, who made tractors there until the early 1980s. The factory was demolished in 1983 and the site is now a large retail park dominated by a Morrison's supermarket and a drive-in MacDonald's.

Right: New Jowett models of light car displayed in a colourful magazine advertisement from 1953.

The Javelin now has the new Series III engine which retains the Javelin's well proved horizontally opposed principle but incorporates the modifications resulting from five years of successful international competition work and from strenuous overseas use. The Jupiter also has the Series III engine tuned for specially high performance — and behind the driver is a roomy tonneau and luggage boot. The Bradford Commercial range— van, utility, and lorry, is known all over the world for its amazing economy and sturdy reliability. These three cars come from the same famous Yorkshire stable of Jowett Cars Limited who have been making cars for nearly half a century.

JOWETT of BRADFORD

ETT CARS LIMITED, IDLE, BRADFORD AND 48 ALBEMARLE STREET, PICCADILLY, LONDON, W.1.

Above: Mountaineer Sir Edmund Hillary, with Lady Hillary, at the wheel of a Jowett Jupiter, at the Earls Court Motor Show, 20th October, 1953.

Above: More than 23,000 units of the streamlined Jowett Javelin Saloon were built between 1947 and 1953 (this model).

HOUSE OF THE YORKSHIRE RIPPER

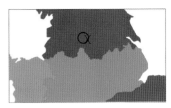

53° 48' 49" N, 1° 47' 24" W

1977–1981

6 GARDEN LANE, HEATON, BRADFORD, WEST YORKSHIRE, BD9 5QJ

PETER SUTCLIFFE'S BRADFORD HOME

It would be ghoulish to produce a litany of murder scenes on a journey around Britain featuring places that have made the news. However, it would be odd to ignore one of the most notorious murder cases in 20th-century history and the place that, curiously, came to symbolise it. Perhaps strangely, it is the home of Peter Sutcliffe, the 'Yorkshire Ripper', rather than the places where he committed the murders, that holds a macabre, but undeniable fascination.

Sutcliffe moved into 6 Garden Lane in the Bradford suburb of Heaton in November 1977 with his wife Sonia. His killing spree had already begun. Sutcliffe's first known victim was Wilma McCann, whom he attacked in Leeds in October 1975. As Sutcliffe continued his murderous activities, it was to this ordinary family house in a comfortable part of Bradford that he would return. Neighbours have spoken since of suspecting him after seeing him burning clothes on bonfires in the garden.

GRUESOME TALLY

Sutcliffe was eventually to be convicted of 13 murders between 1975 and 1980. He also attacked seven other women who survived. It is believed that other unsolved murders and attacks may also have been the work of Sutcliffe, who claimed that he heard voices from God telling him to attack women. Most, but not all, of his victims were working as prostitutes.

Left: Peter Sutcliffe, who claimed that voices from God had told him to attack and kill women.

The Yorkshire Ripper case was a major news story not just in Britain, but around the world in the late 1970s. The case caused widespread fear among women across the North of England for a period of several years. The police had interviewed Sutcliffe on numerous occasions as a suspect, but had failed to link him to the crimes until he was arrested in Sheffield in January 1981 and confessed under questioning. Sutcliffe was sentenced to 20 terms of life imprisonment in 1981. He has been told that he will never be freed from prison.

Sonia Sutcliffe continued to live in the marital home in Bradford for many years. She moved out when she remarried after divorcing Sutcliffe, and her mother lived there for a time, before her death. In 2005, Sonia Sutcliffe moved back in and, at the time of writing, was living there as something of a recluse. The property is still jointly owned by the couple, although it is understood that the Legal Aid Trust would seek to recover Peter Sutcliffe's share of any sale proceeds if the house were sold.

Left: A policeman stands guard outside the detached home of Peter Sutcliffe, 'The Yorkshire Ripper', and his wife Sonia, in Garden Lane, Bradford, on 16th March, 1981. Sutcliffe was arrested on 2nd January, 1981 and charged with 13 counts of murder between 1975 and 1980. On 16th July, 2010 his sentence was extended to a full life term.

BRADFORD CITY
INFERNO

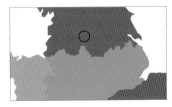

53° 48' 13" N, 1° 45' 38" W

11TH MAY, 1985

VALLEY PARADE, BRADFORD, WEST YORKSHIRE, BD8 7DY

56 FANS KILLED IN A STADIUM BLAZE

Above: The fire at Valley Parade, Bradford, which claimed the lives of 56 people. Litter, ignited by a dropped cigarette, is thought to have caused the blaze.

As you travel along Manningham Lane or Canal Road in Bradford and catch a glimpse of the towering modern stands that now make up Valley Parade, the home of Bradford City Football Club, it's a far cry from the ground that witnessed one of the worst sporting tragedies in British history on a windy afternoon in May 1985.

It should have been a day of celebration for Bradford City and their supporters. They had already secured promotion from what was then Division Three of the Football League. Before the final game of the season – at home to Lincoln City – they were presented with the Trophy and the fans were in celebratory mood. The crowd of over 11,000 people was almost double the average for the season and they were there to celebrate Bradford's first trophy for over half a century.

It was almost half-time, with the score 0–0, when the fire was first noticed. A glow was spotted and spectators sitting in the main stand felt warmth below their feet. Smoke billowed up and the flames took hold. The roof caught fire and the whole stand was in flames within four minutes. Some of those who tried to escape through the exits at the back of the stand found them locked. Most who survived did so by escaping on to the pitch. The fire brigade were on the scene very quickly, but by the time they arrived, the stand was ablaze. Fifty-six people died and at least 265 were injured.

The Bradford City fire would, of course, have been major news in any event, but its impact was magnified because television cameras were there recording the game for a football highlights programme on Yorkshire Television. Within minutes, pictures of the unfolding disaster were being shown live. A local radio reporter, Tony Delahunty, was broadcasting live from inside the stand and his description of what was happening before he fled his commentary position has become one of the most dramatic pieces of radio commentary ever broadcast.

DEADLY LITTER

It is believed that the fire was caused by a lighted cigarette dropped through the floor of the stand, which ignited rubbish that had accumulated for years below the stand floor. The official inquiry, under Mr Justice Popplewell, found that the club had been warned about the dangers of the build-up of litter below the floor of the wooden stand, but had been unable to afford to replace the structure. The Popplewell Inquiry made a number of safety recommendations, including the prohibition of the building of any new wooden stands at sports grounds in Britain.

An appeal for the victims of the fire eventually raised over £3.5m. The most memorable fundraising event was a replaying of the 1966 World Cup Final between England and West Germany, with the original players taking part. It took place at Elland Road in Leeds two months after the fire.

Valley Parade dated back to 1886, when it began its life as the home of Manningham Rugby Club and had been home to Bradford City since 1903. After the fire, it was closed for more than a year. Bradford City played their home games at Elland Road, Leeds, at Leeds Road in Huddersfield and at Bradford's Rugby League ground of Odsal, until Valley Parade reopened in December 1986.

The ground was subsequently further redeveloped when Bradford City enjoyed a brief spell in the Premier League. Today it is entirely transformed from the stadium that suffered such a terrible fate in 1985.

There are two memorials to remember those who died in the fire – one at the end of the stand where the fire started and the other by the main entrance of the ground. Each year at 11 o'clock on the 11th May a small service of remembrance is held in the centre of Bradford. Representatives from Lincoln, Bradford's opponents on the day of the fire, attend the service each year.

Above: The charred remains of the stand at Valley Parade after the tragic blaze. The wooden structure took just minutes to be engulfed in flames.

Above: Bradford City FC chairman Stafford Heginbotham (L) with Mr Justice Popplewell at the start of the inquiry into the blaze.

BELLE VUE
MANCHESTER

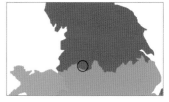

53° 27' 44" N, 2° 11' 1" W

1836–1987

BELLE VUE STADIUM, KIRKMANSHULME LANE, MANCHESTER, M18 7BD

ONCE THE NORTH OF ENGLAND'S GREATEST PLEASURE PARK COMPLEX

Above: The Belle Vue Gardens and the Amusement Park, with the Floral Clock at the entrance, on 17th June, 1946. Looming over the scene is the roller coaster known as the 'Bobs', said to refer to the original cost of a ride, which was one shilling, or a 'bob'. It had an 80-foot drop at a 45-degree angle, down which the cars travelled at 60 miles per hour.

Above: The official 1947 guide to The New Belle Vue leisure park boasted that it was the 'showground of the world'.

also created by the Victorians, places such as Belle Vue were the 'lungs' of the city, providing leisure and recreation facilities as a relief from the grind of life in industrial towns.

MASS APPEAL

Belle Vue began life in 1836 as a series of formal gardens, where the Manchester middle classes could enjoy genteel pleasures. An aviary and then a zoo were part of the early years of Belle Vue. The founder, John Jennison, was primarily interested in the horticultural and zoological aspects of the park, but over the years, facing financial pressures, he added amusements and the park's character changed. It was no longer the preserve of the middle classes, but largely thanks to the arrival of the railway, it became a place where the working classes also flocked in great numbers.

Belle Vue boasted regular and impressive fireworks displays, and was a venue for circuses. It had a boating lake, dodgems, a ghost train and a scenic railway. The King's Hall, opened in 1910, was a major concert and exhibition venue. The Halle Orchestra played there regularly for many years. In a sense, there was something for everyone.

At its height Belle Vue was attracting over two million visitors a year, including up to 250,000 during the Easter weekend alone. In a more innocent age, the pleasures and thrills available at Belle Vue were attractive and convenient for a population that was still largely reliant on public transport.

FAST TRACKS

Sport became a regular part of Belle Vue in 1926, with the opening of a greyhound stadium and three years later with the building of a speedway stadium – once reckoned to be the largest in the world. It became the home of the Belle Vue Aces, one of the most famous names in speedway. The stadium continued until 1987, but it was demolished and the speedway team returned to the greyhound stadium, although there are plans for a new speedway stadium due to open in 2013.

Broughton Rangers Rugby League team, later renamed Belle Vue Rangers, played at the speedway stadium for some years. There was a very short-lived

Belle Vue was quite simply a theme park from an earlier age. In its heyday it was on a scale that matched or bettered any other similar pleasure park in Britain. Yet today, there is nothing of substance left of this once mighty venue apart from a greyhound and speedway track and a snooker hall.

Belle Vue, like The Crystal Palace in London and Bellahouston Park in Glasgow, was a product of the Victorian age. It was a place, then located on the outskirts of town, that provided leisure activities for the burgeoning population of a great industrial conurbation. Alongside the great municipal parks

Left: Lil, an Indian elephant, arrived at Belle Vue Zoological Gardens in 1921 accompanied by her British Malayan handler, Phil Fernandez. The pair provided much-loved entertainment, advertising, and popular elephant rides, until Lil died in 1947. Fernandez remained at Belle Vue until his death in 1956.

experiment with football – a team named Manchester Central, based at Belle Vue, tried to get into the Football League in the early 1930s, but folded in 1934.

Immediately after the Second World War, Belle Vue was still thriving as the leisure industry enjoyed a post-war boom, with people looking for distractions from the struggles of wartime and the rationing and austerity of the late 1940s.

CARS AND COMPETITION

However, from the 1950s onwards, with rival amusement parks opening up and the expansion in car ownership widening people's horizons, the slow decline of Belle Vue was probably inevitable. British caterer and hotelier Charles Forte bought Belle Vue in 1956 and made some investments, but there was a serious fire in 1958, which destroyed many of the buildings.

In the end Belle Vue's death was a long, lingering one. The zoo closed in 1977 and the animals were sold. The Amusement Park survived until 1982, but was then demolished and the land sold off.

The King's Hall, which had been the largest exhibition space outside London, suffered from increasing competition. The opening of a new venue in central Manchester, then called G-Mex, now Manchester Central, in 1986, was the final straw. The King's Hall closed in 1987. The site of the Hall is now occupied by a car auction business.

The greyhound and speedway stadium and snooker hall are the only real remains. There's a tenpin bowling alley on the filled-in site where Belle Vue's Great Lake stood. The rest of the 165 acres once occupied by Belle Vue is now largely housing and small industrial units. One of the streets on the former site is named Lockhart Close, after the circus master George Lockhart.

Belle Vue is still regarded with enormous affection by many Mancunians. In recent years there has been a local campaign to create a linear park that would partly include some land within what was once Belle Vue. However, unlike many other venues that were once great places of public resort, Belle Vue did not manage to reinvent itself for another great public purpose and there is very little discernible trace of a place where millions once flocked to enjoy themselves.

Left: Belle Vue's undulating 'Bug' ride was just one of the many entertainments offered to visitors to the popular Manchester amusement park.

Left: The larger Belle Vue's boating lake was created in 1858 and was known as the Great Lake. Located in the Hyde Road, Kirkmanshulme Lane corner of the park, it was fed with water from the Stockport Branch Canal. The original lake was round. In 1876 it was made pear shaped, bringing it closer to the Lake Hotel. In 1882 an island was created and a prominent clock tower was added.

MANCHESTER
FREE TRADE
HALL

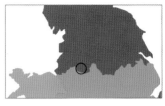

53° 28' 40" N, 2° 14' 47" W

1853–1997

RADISSON HOTEL, PETER STREET, MANCHESTER, M2 5GP

A GREAT MANCHESTER CONCERT HALL ON THE SITE OF THE PETERLOO MASSACRE

Above: The façade of the Free Trade Hall on Peter Street is all that survives of the original 1853–56 building. The rear, post-war reconstruction of the main hall was itself demolished and replaced by a 263-bedroom hotel in glass and stone.

Above: A plaque commemorating the Peterloo Massacre was unveiled on 10th September, 2007, on the surviving façade of the Free Trade Hall.

Right: Mr H. Sherwood Edwards working on a section of his Peterloo mural, which was to be hung in the Free Trade Hall in 1951.

M any of the locations featured in this journey have disappeared without a fight or with little or no opposition. The Free Trade Hall is an exception. Manchester's concert hall, and the home of the Hallé Orchestra for almost a century and a half, is still mourned by those who remember it. Perhaps one reason for the affection is that the Free Trade Hall hosted such a diverse range of events over its history and that it stood on a site charged with such political significance.

The land where the Free Trade Hall was built in the 1850s had been the scene of one of the defining political events of 19th-century Britain. Fifteen people died and more than 400, perhaps as many as 700, were injured when cavalry charged a demonstration held in August 1819 to demand better political representation and an end to the highly unpopular Corn Laws. The events produced a deep sense of shock across the country, led in the short term to a hard-line response from the Government, but eventually resulted in political reform and the repeal of the Corn Laws.

The Free Trade Hall was built between 1853 and 1856 on what had been Peter's Field, where the massacre took place. It was built to commemorate the repeal of the Corn Laws and was funded by public subscription. It became a concert hall and home of the Hallé in 1858. In 1920 it was taken over by Manchester Corporation. During the Second World War, it was badly damaged in the Manchester Blitz, but was reopened in 1951.

Throughout its history the Free Trade Hall played host to great political events, to great classical musicians, but also to rock and pop stars. Among the politicians who spoke there were Benjamin Disraeli and Winston Churchill. The suffragettes Christabel Pankhurst and Annie Kenney were ejected from the Hall in 1905, when they interrupted a political meeting as part of the campaign for votes for women.

HOME OF THE HALLÉ

The internationally-acclaimed English contralto, Kathleen Ferrier, performed at the reopening after the wartime bombing of the Free Trade Hall, on the 16th November, 1951. She sang *Land of Hope and*

Above: Queen Elizabeth, The Queen Mother unveils a commemorative tablet at the Free Trade Hall, on its reopening after rebuilding to repair bomb damage suffered during the war, on 16th November, 1951.

Above: Members of The Hallé Orchestra stand to honour Sir John Barbirolli as he leaves the stage of the Free Trade Hall after his last performance on 29th May, 1968.

Glory as the finale of the concert, even though she was already undergoing treatment for breast cancer, which was to kill her at an early age less than two years later.

The classical music figure most closely associated with the Free Trade Hall was Sir John Barbirolli, who led the Hallé as its principal conductor from 1943 until his death in 1970. He is widely credited with having revived the fortunes of the orchestra.

ROCK LEGENDS

However, it wasn't only classical music that resounded through the Free Trade Hall. Among those who performed there were Bob Dylan, The Rolling Stones, Pink Floyd, Genesis, Jethro Tull and Black Sabbath. The Sex Pistols played at the Lesser Free Trade Hall (a

smaller auditorium at the main hall) twice in 1976, at concerts that have entered the folklore of popular music history and which are often seen as instrumental in the birth of punk rock.

By the 1990s, however, the Free Trade Hall was deemed to be unfit for a city with Manchester's ambition, and a new concert hall, the Bridgewater Hall, was built nearby. The Hallé moved there in 1996 and Manchester City Council closed the Free Trade Hall in 1997, selling it to private developers, despite some local opposition.

After several years of wrangling the building was eventually converted into a hotel, which opened at a cost of £45m in 2004. The façade of the original building on Peter Street has been retained, but the remainder of the building was demolished, although some of the artefacts from the Free Trade Hall are preserved in the new building.

Above: Rock band The Rolling Stones during their concert at The Free Trade Hall on 5th March,1971. The Stones were just one of many rock and pop acts to grace the stage of the hall.

Above: Prefects, staff and visiting dignitaries on stage at the annual speech day of the Hollies FCJ School, in the 1970s. The event was held at the hall from the beginning of the 1960s until it closed in the 1990s.

Above: Memorabilia of concerts held at the Free Trade Hall is prized by collectors, such as this programme and ticket stubs for a performance of the J. Geils Band on 2nd June, 1980.

Above: Sir John Barbirolli and the Hallé Orchestra test the acoustics in advance of a concert celebrating the reopening of the rebuilt Free Trade Hall, in November 1951.

ROYAL OLDHAM
HOSPITAL

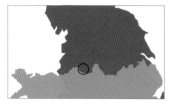

53° 33' 10" N, 2° 7' 16" W

25TH JULY, 1978 — ROYAL OLDHAM HOSPITAL, ROCHDALE ROAD, OLDHAM, GREATER MANCHESTER, OL1 2JH

THE WORLD'S FIRST TEST-TUBE BABY IS BORN

Above: On 26th July, 1978 consultant gynaecologist Patrick Steptoe (seated, R) and Dr Robert Edwards (seated, L) at Oldham General Hospital held a press conference to announce the long-anticipated birth of the world's first test-tube baby the previous day.

Shortly before midnight on Tuesday, 25th July, 1978 a baby girl was delivered by caesarean section at what was then the Oldham General Hospital. However, the arrival of Louise Brown was no ordinary birth. She was the first person in the world to be born by IVF, in vitro fertilisation, and became known as the world's first test-tube baby.

Louise's parents, Lesley and John Brown, had been trying unsuccessfully for a baby for nine years. However, Lesley suffered from blocked fallopian tubes. In November 1977 she underwent an operation conducted by the obstetrician Patrick Steptoe and the biologist Robert Edwards, who had been working together since Steptoe had founded the Centre for

Human Reproduction in Oldham in 1969. Before Louise Brown was born there had been a number of unsuccessful attempts at achieving in vitro fertilisation over a period of several years. Throughout the summer of 1978 there was enormous media interest in the impending arrival, and Louise's birth became a cloak-and-dagger operation.

SECRET CAESAREAN

The Browns lived in Bristol, but they went into hiding in Lincoln at Patrick Steptoe's mother's house. When the birth was imminent, reporters tried to sneak into Lesley Brown's room in the hospital in Oldham. Even at the last minute Steptoe tried to keep the birth a secret by bringing the day of the caesarean operation forward to try to confuse the press.

However, once Louise was safely delivered and was pronounced healthy, the IVF pioneers were keen to publicise their achievement and the world's first test-tube baby was headline news around the world. Steptoe and Edwards were the subject of criticism from some religious leaders, who saw their work as meddling with nature.

FERTILITY CLINIC

Steptoe founded the Bourn Hall Clinic in Cambridgeshire in 1980 as a centre of expertise for infertility treatments. By 2012 there had been an estimated four million IVF births worldwide and there were around 30,000 IVF births in Britain each year.

Louise's younger sister, Natalie, was also born by IVF four years later. In 1999, she became the first IVF baby to give birth to her own child, and Louise also became a mother in 2006. Lesley Brown, the woman who had given birth to the world's first IVF baby, died in 2012 at the age of 64.

Patrick Steptoe died in 1988, but Robert Edwards was awarded a Nobel Prize in 2010. Oldham General Hospital was later renamed the Royal Oldham Hospital. There are two plaques commemorating the event – one near the operating theatre and the other outside the maternity unit. In 2012 plans were under way to relocate the maternity unit, but the operating theatre where Louise's birth took place is still in use.

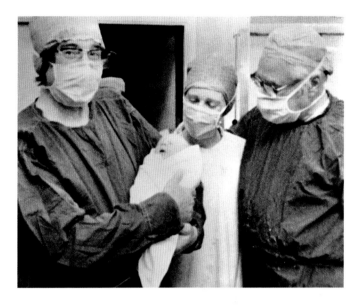

Above: Dr Robert Edwards holds baby Louise Joy Brown, the world's first test-tube baby, watched by the midwife and Patrick Steptoe. Louise was born by planned caesarian section, weighing 5lb 12oz.

Above: Louise Brown from Bristol, the world's first IVF baby, at the 30th anniversary celebration of her birth, held at the Bourn Hall Clinic, Bourn, Cambridgeshire, on 12th July, 2008.

BURNDEN PARK
BOLTON

53° 34' 9" N, 2° 24' 56" W

9TH MARCH, 1946

BURNDEN PARK, BOLTON, GREATER MANCHESTER, BL3 2QS

33 FANS DIE IN FOOTBALL STADIUM CRUSH

More recent events – notably at Bradford City and at Hillsborough – have rather eclipsed the name of Burnden Park from the list of stadium disasters that has afflicted the national game. However, on the afternoon of 9th March, 1946, the former ground of Bolton Wanderers was the scene of one of the worst disasters in the game's history. The loss of life, the circumstances of the disaster and the way the events were handled all marked this out as one of the most significant sporting tragedies in British history.

This was the first season of football after the Second World War and the match was an FA Cup Quarter Final Second Leg game between Bolton Wanderers and Stoke City. At the time people mainly stood at football matches rather than sitting and entry was by paying at the turnstiles rather than buying tickets in advance. It is estimated that as many as 85,000 were crammed into a ground whose capacity pre-war had been around 70,000. However, the real capacity was lower, as part of the ground was closed because the Ministry of Supply, which had taken it over during the war, had not yet handed it back.

The trouble happened at the Railway End, which was a rough bank of dirt terracing. The signs were ominous before the kick-off and officials, fearing serious overcrowding, had shut off the turnstiles in that part of the ground 20 minutes earlier. However, fans continued to pour in from the railway and over the turnstiles. Shortly after kick-off, fans started invading the pitch to escape the overcrowded terrace. Two barriers collapsed and people fell forward, crushing those below them. The game was stopped once it was clear there were fatalities.

MATCH RESUMED

Astonishingly, as bodies piled up on the touchline covered by coats, the players came back out after half an hour and the game was resumed, being played out to a goalless draw. It was obvious to spectators elsewhere in the ground that something serious had happened, although the scale of the disaster was not apparent to most of them until they went home and heard the full facts on the radio.

In total 33 people died that day and several hundred were injured. The official inquiry made a number of recommendations, including safety inspections by local authorities, crowd limits and the installation of internal phone systems at grounds.

Before the tragedy of 1946, Burnden Park had been home to Bolton Wanderers since 1895 and had witnessed many great games, including hosting the

FA Cup Final Replay in 1901. Throughout the first half of the 20th century Bolton were one of the most successful clubs in English football, and Burnden Park witnessed the skills of Nat Lofthouse and many other great players.

However, in the latter years of the century, Burnden Park's fortunes mirrored the struggle of the club itself. Bolton slipped through the divisions; attendances declined and the ground was increasingly decrepit, unnecessarily large and clearly uneconomic. In 1986 part of the Railway End, the area where the disaster occurred, was sold off to allow the building of a Normid supermarket.

The income from this venture was a short-lived stay of execution for the grand old ground. In 1992, the directors decided to leave Burnden Park – a dream that was finally achieved five years later with the move to the Reebok Stadium on the north-west outskirts of Bolton.

The new ground is part of a retail and leisure development and the site of the old ground is likewise. A supermarket on the site includes a commemoration of Bolton Wanderers' use of Burnden Park for 102 years. As with so many places on this journey, where once history was made, people now do their shopping.

Facing page: The FA Cup Final Replay between Tottenham Hotspur and Sheffield United, at Burnden Park on 27th April, 1901. Spurs became the only non-league side to win the FA Cup when they beat Sheffield United 3–1 before an attendance of 20,470.

Left: The tragic scene at Burnden Park, where 33 fans were crushed to death after an estimated crowd of 85,000 crammed into the 65,000-capacity ground.

PARK HOSPITAL
DAVYHULME

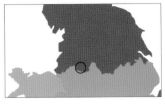

53° 27' 8" N, 2° 22' 14" W

5TH JULY, 1948   TRAFFORD GENERAL HOSPITAL, MOORSIDE ROAD, DAVYHULME, GREATER MANCHESTER, M41 5SL

WHERE BRITAIN'S NATIONAL HEALTH SERVICE WAS BORN

Above: Nurses formed a 'guard of honour' for Health Minister Aneurin Bevan when he arrived at Park Hospital, Davyhulme, near Manchester, to mark the launch of Britain's National Health Service, on 5th July, 1948.

Above: Aneurin Bevan meets the first-ever NHS patient, 13-year-old Sylvia Beckingham, the youngest person on Ward 5 at the Park Hospital, Davyhulme, watched by nurses.

Above: Renamed Trafford General Hospital in 1988, and subsequently redeveloped, many of the buildings, including the distinctive clock tower, still remain, as shown in this photograph of 2nd April, 2012.

On Monday, 5th July, 1948 the Health Minister in the post-war Labour Government, Aneurin Bevan, ceremonially took possession of Park Hospital in Davyhulme near Manchester from Lancashire County Council to mark the start of the National Health Service. Nurses formed a guard of honour when Bevan arrived and he was handed the keys of the hospital as a symbol of the creation of one of the most significant social reforms of 20th-century Britain.

FIRST NHS PATIENTS

It's not known why Park Hospital was chosen to be the place where the advent of the NHS was marked, although it's believed that there was a connection between the managers of the hospital and senior government figures. Bevan visited Ward 5 and spoke to the NHS's first patient, 13-year-old Sylvia Beckingham. She was being accommodated on an adult ward because there had been an outbreak of measles on the children's ward. Sandra Pook, born at the hospital that day, weighing 6lb 11oz, was the first baby delivered by the NHS.

The creation of the NHS was included as one of the recommendations of the Beveridge Report in 1942, which is widely seen as the blueprint for the welfare state created by the Labour Government after its election victory in 1945. The idea of health treatment free at the point of delivery predated Beveridge. Prior to the Second World War, it existed in some places and was provided for certain people. During the war, a Government-run Emergency Medical Service was a forerunner of the NHS and there appeared to be a widespread consensus that post-war Britain should adopt a national health service.

However, despite earlier supporting the idea, doctors voted to oppose it and their opposition threatened to derail the whole scheme. In a phrase for which he became famous, Bevan had "to stuff their mouths with gold" to get them to agree. Within two years of the start of the NHS, costs were escalating well beyond expectations and the first prescription charges were introduced.

More than 60 years later the NHS remains after many reforms. It enjoys widespread support, but its future and its organisation remain a source of political controversy. Park Hospital was renamed Trafford General Hospital in 1988. There have been extensive redevelopments on the site, but the buildings where Bevan arrived are still there. A plaque near the main information desk commemorates the events of 1948 and the history of the hospital is told in boards on the hospital walls.

In 2008, on the 60th anniversary of the foundation of the NHS, patients and staff from the pioneering early days were invited back for a special celebration.

LIVERPOOL GARDEN
FESTIVAL

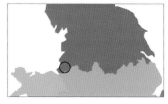

53° 22' 35" N, 2° 58' 7" W

2ND MAY–14TH OCTOBER, 1984   FESTIVAL GARDENS, RIVERSIDE DRIVE, LIVERPOOL, L3 4AZ

A 1980s REGENERATION PROJECT ITSELF
REGENERATED

Above: The Festival Gardens site shortly after opening in 1984. It was split into 60 separate gardens and occupied a derelict industrial area.

The Liverpool International Garden Festival symbolises the 1980s in so many ways – industrial dereliction, optimistic political intervention and leisure-based regeneration. However, the site where the Festival took place as an act of regeneration had itself been subject to further dereliction once the crowds had departed.

The Festival was the first of a series of five major garden festivals held in the 1980s and 1990s in Britain – Stoke, Glasgow, Ebbw Vale and Gateshead being the others. It is credited as having been the brainchild of the then Conservative Environment Secretary, Michael Heseltine, as a means of helping the regeneration of Liverpool. The city had suffered greatly from the decline of its port and other industries. The site chosen for the festival was a derelict industrial area, part of which had

been a refuse dump near the old Herculaneum Dock.

Michael Heseltine championed the idea of the festival as a way of kick-starting Liverpool's recovery from industrial decline, by attracting tourists and to help change its image. The project was not without its critics, some of whom saw it as a rather temporary and fluffy response to more deep-seated economic problems.

ORIENTAL THEME

The festival, however, proved to be very popular with more than three million visitors during the five months it was open. The main attractions included 60 individual gardens. Perhaps the best known were the Japanese Gardens and pagodas. The centrepiece of the site was

Above: Blue Peter *presenter Simon Groom and Goldie the labrador meet Queen Elizabeth II and the Duke of Edinburgh in the Blue Peter Garden, when the Queen opened Liverpool's International Garden Festival on 2nd May, 1984.*

Above: The 18-ton steel Yellow Submarine made famous in the 1966 Beatles song, built at the Cammell Laird Shipyard, is towed across the Mersey by barge to be placed at the heart of the Beatles Maze, a highlight of the festival.

LIVERPOOL INTERNATIONAL GARDEN FESTIVAL 1984

Above: A postcard of the Liverpool International Garden Festival, 1984.

INTERNATIONAL GA

KEY TO MAP

National Themes
1 Seven Seas Garden
2 Tree Council Garden
3 Liverpool Street
4 Liverpool Quiz
5 Witch Garden
6 Sculpture Terraces
7 Picnic Area
8 Jam Garden
9 Beatles Maze
10 Blue Peter Garden
11 Promenade Garden
12 Heather and Conifer Garden
13 Granada Television
14 Alpine Garden
15 Rose Garden
16 Garden of Hope
17 Victorian Garden
18 Snakes in the Grass
19 The Water Margin
20 Rock Garden
21 Land Treatment Maze
22 Grass Garden
23 Plantsman's Corner
24 Scottish Garden
25 Vine Garden
26 Organic Garden
27 Allotments Garden
28 Kitchen Garden
29 Nursery Garden
30 Sculptor's Corner
31 Model Forest
32 Gardens for Disabled Persons

33 Gardening is for Everyone
34 Nature Garden
35 Wild Garden
36 Wild Plants We Use
37 New Lands for Old

International Themes
38 Austria
39 France
40 Great Britain
41 Canada
42 Belgium
43 Egypt
44 Greece
45 Spain
46 Australia
47 'The Australian Bicentenary 1788-1988'
48 Portugal
49 Turkey
50 Federal Republic of Germany
51 United Kingdom Government Pavilion
52 Italy
53 Holland
54 Japan
55 United States of America
56 The People's Republic of China
57 Cologne
58 India

Home and Garden Feature
A Ceramic Garden

B Abbey National Building Society
C Broseley Estates Ltd.
D Wimpey Homes Holdings Ltd.
E Barratt Northern Ltd.
F Barratt Northern Ltd.
G Cheshire Garden
H National Garden Festival Stoke on Trent
J Canal Garden
K Norwest Holst (V.I.P. Suite)

Herculaneum Entrance:
Toilets; Telephone;
Lost Property;
Post Office; First Aid;
Lost Children;
Buttery;
Information;
Left Luggage;
Souvenir Shop;
(Wheelchairs available).

Fulwood Entrance:
Bank;
Toilets;
Telephone;
Lost Property;
First Aid;
Buttery;
Information;
Left Luggage;
Souvenir Shop;
(Wheelchairs available).

▲ Photog Points
□ Theme

HERCULANEUM CAR PARK

the massive Festival Hall, which contained a series of exhibits and events. There was a miniature railway around the site, which borrowed engines and rolling stock from other narrow-gauge railways in Britain.

After the festival ended, the Festival Hall became the Pleasure Island Amusement Park from the late 1980s until 1996. A large area of the site was turned into housing, but much of the site remained derelict for over a decade after the amusement park closed.

RESTORATION SCHEME

Eventually, permission was granted for a scheme to restore part of the original gardens as a public park alongside the building of a further 1,300 homes. There were further delays but, in 2012, after a series of problems, including a contractor going bust, parts of the Garden Festival site were finally due to open again to the public, including the restored Japanese and Chinese Gardens. The plans for more houses were on hold.

The site changed from industrial use to temporary leisure use and then to housing. But its history is also a demonstration of how there's often a desire to retain some part of the original public purpose of a great scheme, in this case the ornamental gardens. So the legacy of the Liverpool Garden Festival will live on almost 30 years after the festival closed.

Above: The Nursery Garden contained a variety of features to appeal to young children.

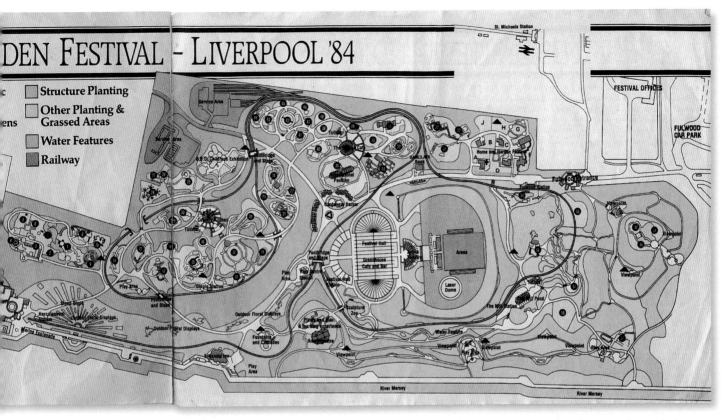

DEN FESTIVAL - LIVERPOOL '84

Structure Planting

Other Planting & Grassed Areas

Water Features

Railway

Above: A map of the festival site listed the 60 individual gardens and the facilities for visitors, which included a miniature railway, buttery and souvenir shop.

Above: The Oriental pagodas, seen here shortly after the site opened, were very popular with the visitors to the Festival Gardens.

Above: The Festival Gardens were refurbished in 2011, thanks to a £3.7m grant from the Northwest Regional Development Agency. When the 1984 festival ended, part of the site was developed into residential housing, while the remainder fell into disrepair in the late 1990s.

THE
CAVERN CLUB
LIVERPOOL

53° 24' 22" N, 2° 59' 15" W

9TH FEBRUARY, 1961

10 MATHEW STREET, LIVERPOOL, L2 6RE

THE BIRTHPLACE OF THE BEATLES

Above: Popular Merseybeat band The Escorts, who were active between 1962 and 1966, with various changes in line-up, perform beneath the arches in The Cavern Club in 1964.

Above: Ray McFall, who bought the Cavern Club from the original owner, Alan Synter, in 1959, was forced to close it in February 1966 when he could not afford essential renovations.

Many of the places on this journey might be rightly considered iconic, but most don't flaunt it – some for obvious reasons. At The Cavern Club in Liverpool, they flaunt it in spades and with some justification. On 9th February, 1961, The Beatles first performed at the club (although they had been performing at other venues since August 1960). They went on to play at The Cavern almost 300 times in the next two years. Even though they never played there as a group after 1963, The Cavern is still regarded as their spiritual home.

The Cavern Club had opened in 1957 and in its first few years was mainly a jazz club. But skiffle groups including the Quarry Men, featuring both John Lennon (7th August, 1957) and Paul McCartney (24th January, 1958), played there from the first year of the club's existence. Then, in February 1961, the group first performed there under their new name of The Beatles, having returned from a tour of Hamburg. The line-up was John Lennon, Paul McCartney and George Harrison with Stuart Sutcliffe and Pete Best. Sutcliffe left the band and returned to Hamburg shortly after the first Cavern gig.

Above: The famous stage within the modern-day Cavern Club celebrates the Liverpool venue's connection with the legendary Fab Four.

Later that year a local record shop owner, Brian Epstein, saw them play at The Cavern and offered to become their manager. It was Epstein who secured them a record deal with George Martin the following year.

REFLECTED GLORY

Between the first gig and their last on 3rd August 1963, The Beatles played a remarkable 292 times at The Cavern. By then, though, they were internationally known and The Cavern wasn't big enough for the audiences the group could now command. Epstein's promise to bring The Beatles back to The Cavern was never fulfilled.

The Cavern basked in the reflected glory of the Beatles and many famous groups and solo artists played there, including The Hollies, The Kinks, The Rolling Stones and The Who. Cilla Black worked there as a cloakroom attendant. However, in February 1966 financial problems forced its closure for a few months, but it was reopened under new owners by the then

Prime Minister, Harold Wilson, on 23rd July, 1966. In its new manifestation it had a souvenir shop, a coffee bar, an eatery and a boutique.

In the early 1970s artists like Queen, Status Quo and Suzi Quatro appeared there, but in 1973 The Cavern was closed when British Rail acquired the site as part of the extension of the Merseyrail system. The converted cellars which were the heart of the club were filled in with rubble. The club reopened across the street, but changed its name a couple of times before folding.

CAVERN REBORN

It was in 1984 that The Cavern Club was reborn. A consortium involving the former Liverpool footballer, Tommy Smith, spearheaded the redevelopment of part of the original site. This new Cavern, complete with a replica of the original club, opened on 26th April, 1984. Many of the bricks from the original club were reused in the new development. There have been various changes of ownership and management since then and there was a period of closure from 1989 to 1991 after the club lost its licence. Since then The Cavern has been a mainstream part of the Liverpool tourist experience as well as continuing as a live music venue.

Although The Beatles never returned to The Cavern as a group, Ringo Starr has been back and Paul McCartney's most famous return visit was on 14th December, 1999 when he was there as part of a Millennium tour with thousands also watching the concert live in the middle of Liverpool on a big screen.

Above: The Cavern Club in February 1966, during its period of enforced closure. It reopened on 11th May, 1966 under new management.

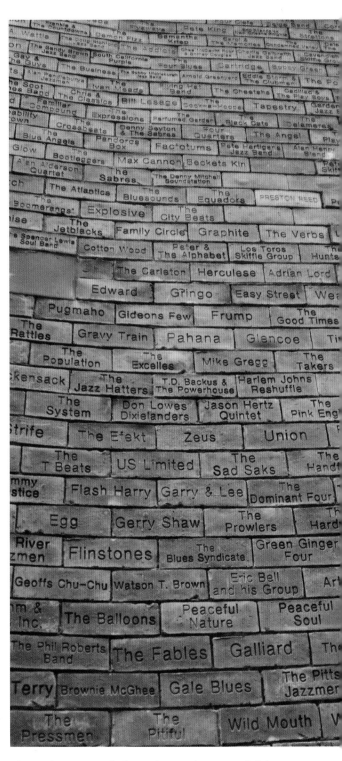

Above: The Cavern Wall of Fame features the names of all the artists who have appeared at the iconic venue.

Above: The entrance to the new Cavern Club, still at the forefront of Liverpool's live music circuit.

LIVERPOOL
OVERHEAD RAILWAY

53° 23' 6" N, 2° 57' 55" W

30TH DECEMBER, 1956   ROSCOE ENGINEERING, PARK ROAD, LIVERPOOL, L8 9RF

CLOSURE OF A UNIQUE RAILWAY SERVICE

Above: An electric train on Liverpool's unique overhead railway passes one of the entrances to the Mersey Tunnel, on 5th May, 1946.

Thousands of former railway stations, railway lines and other railway structures litter the British landscape, both urban and rural. Most of those relics of the railway were rendered obsolete during the Beeching cuts. In Liverpool, however, the curtain came down earlier than that on a unique piece of Britain's railway heritage.

On the evening of Sunday, 30th December, 1956, the last trains ran on the Liverpool Overhead Railway, which had operated along the dock front for 63 years. Known affectionately as the 'Dockers' Umbrella', it ran for most of its length on an elevated platform along the waterfront under which dockers could shelter as they moved around the port.

WORLD FIRST

When it opened in 1893, it was the first elevated electric railway in the world and it was the first to use automatic signalling and electric signals. Its other claim to fame was that it was the first to use electric multiple units and therefore did not require separate locomotives.

The railway ran for a total length of about seven miles from Seaforth and Litherland in the north to Dingle in the south. The most southerly section to Dingle ran through a tunnel.

The railway suffered severe bomb damage during the Second World War, although it was repaired. There was also modernisation of the rolling stock during the 1940s and 1950s. However, there was a need for substantial repairs to the infrastructure of the line. By

Above: A poster offering a round trip on the Overhead Railway shows a somewhat picturesque vision of the route, taking in "unrivalled views of dockland and shipping".

Above: A map showing the principal buildings and Liverpool's famous docks on the route of the Overhead Railway.

1954 it had been estimated that the railway needed to spend £2m (more than £40m at 2012 prices) to carry out all the improvements necessary. The line, however, was owned by a private company – and it couldn't raise the money.

LAST TRAINS RUN

Despite a local campaign to try to save the line and suggestions that it might be taken over by Liverpool City Council or by British Railways, closure was authorised by a special Act of Parliament. Thousands turned out to witness the last trains run as 1956 drew to a close. The demolition of the railway infrastructure started the following September.

The only significant remains of the railway are the tunnel portal at Herculaneum and the remains of Dingle Station in the tunnel section. An engineering firm now uses the station as its premises. In 2011 the newly opened Museum of Liverpool included a gallery about the history of the Liverpool Overhead Railway. The gallery features many artefacts from the railway, including an original carriage and a model showing the route along the docks.

Above: One of the Overhead Railway's electric multiple units – which required no separate locomotive – passes along the track at the level of the rows of housing on the left, at Seaforth Sands.

Above: Viaducts carried the trains over road intersections. Dockers would shelter beneath the elevated sections of the railway while moving about the docks. This photograph is from May 1946.

Above: The Liverpool Overhead Railway passed alongside many of the city's notable buildings, served by stations that were accessible from the lower street level.

Above: A postcard illustrating the Liverpool Overhead Railway and St Nicholas Church.

Left: A poster advertising the connections between the Liverpool Overhead Railway and the Southport branch of the Lancashire & Yorkshire Railway.

Above: One of the Liverpool Overhead Railway carriages on display on an elevated section of track, in the Museum of Liverpool, 2012.

NEW BRIGHTON
TOWER

53° 26' 20" N, 3° 2' 11" W

1896–1969

TOWER PROMENADE, NEW BRIGHTON, WALLASEY, MERSEYSIDE, CH45 2PP

SHORT-LIVED RIVAL TO BLACKPOOL TOWER

E_45323. NEW BRIGHTON,
TOWER & SANDS.

Above: A postcard illustrating New Brighton Tower in all its glory – an edifice to rival the tower in Blackpool. At the end of the First World War, high maintenance costs spelled doom for the spectacular structure.

Many people are unaware that another tower, as well as the famous Blackpool Tower, once graced the coastline of the North West of England. Work began in 1896 to build a tower at the resort of New Brighton, on the Wirral opposite Liverpool. When completed the lattice-steel structure was 567 feet high – some 49 feet higher than its rival in Blackpool.

New Brighton Tower became the focal point for what was then a thriving resort on the Mersey. The tower boasted winter gardens, a ballroom and refreshment room, and four lifts took people to the top for commanding views of the Lancashire and Cheshire coasts, the Isle of Man and the Lake District.

LOFTY IDEAS

The tower was set in extensive grounds that included a fairground, lakes, outdoor dancing platforms and a miniature railway. The Athletic Grounds once staged the World Cycling Championships and were home to two football clubs. In 1896 New Brighton Tower FC was set up as a team to play in a massive stadium that had been built as part of the construction of the tower. The team was elected to the Football League in 1898, but lasted only three seasons, averaging crowds of little more than 1,000 in a stadium that could hold 80,000. However, in the 1920s, another attempt was made to stage football in the grounds with the establishment of New Brighton AFC, who remained as members of the league from

1923 to 1951. At the outbreak of the First World War, New Brighton Tower was closed for military reasons. It soon fell into disrepair and, after the war ended, the owners were unable to afford the repairs to the rusting structure. The tower was dismantled between 1919 and 1921, but the base, including the elegant ballroom, was retained.

For a further 50 years, the ballroom continued to be used and, in the 1950s and 1960s, was a popular rock 'n' roll venue. Among the artists who performed there were Little Richard and, most famously, The Beatles, who played there in November 1961 and on a further 26 occasions. The end came in 1969 when fire destroyed the remaining buildings, including the ballroom. New Brighton Tower was no more. In the 1970s part of the grounds were sold for housing and the rest remains a public park. In 2011 a plaque was unveiled to mark the connection between The Beatles and the former New Brighton Tower ballroom.

Above: The grand ballroom endured after the tower was dismantled and eventually became a popular rock 'n' roll venue in the 1960s, until fire destroyed the building.

Left: A bright future for the spectacular New Brighton Tower and its many attractions came to a sad end (above) on 6th April, 1920, when the famous landmark was in the process of being dismantled.

CARL BRIDGEWATER
SHOOTING
AT YEW TREE FARM

19TH SEPTEMBER, 1978   THE FORMER YEW TREE FARM, PRESTWOOD, STOURBRIDGE, WEST MIDLANDS, DY7 5AW

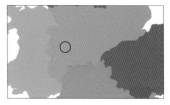

52° 28' 35" N, 2° 11' 31" W

SHOOTING OF A NEWSPAPER BOY AND A MISCARRIAGE OF JUSTICE

Above: Police outside Yew Tree Farm, near Stourbridge, West Midlands, where the body of newspaper boy Carl Bridgewater was found.

On the afternoon of Tuesday, 19th September, 1978 13-year-old Carl Bridgewater was delivering newspapers to what was then called Yew Tree Farm, on the A449 about three miles from Stourbridge. The couple who lived at the farm were out, but Carl went in to investigate when he found the door open. He had disturbed a burglary and was shot dead at point-blank range after being forced into the living room.

UNSAFE CONVICTIONS

After a similar robbery not far away a few weeks later, four men were eventually arrested in connection with Carl's death. Cousins Michael and Vincent Hickey and Jim Robinson were convicted of murder. Robinson and Vincent Hickey were sentenced to 25 years minimum term and Michael Hickey, who was 17, was ordered to be detained at Her Majesty's pleasure. The fourth man,

Patrick Molloy, was found guilty of manslaughter and sentenced to 12 years.

Molloy died in prison of a heart attack in 1981, but in 1997, after a series of earlier appeals, the Court of Appeal overturned the convictions of the 'Bridgewater Four' on the grounds that evidence that had led Molloy to make a confession had been fabricated. The three surviving men were freed and received compensation. The campaign to clear their names had been led by Michael Hickey's mother, Ann Whelan, and campaigning journalist Paul Foot. After his release, Jim Robinson died of cancer in 2007.

Rumours have abounded over the years linking another convicted murderer to the Bridgewater case, but he has denied any involvement. The police have repeatedly said that they have no plans to reopen the case. Carl's parents, Janet and Brian Bridgewater, still live in the area.

For many years Yew Tree Farm was derelict. In 2004 it was refurbished and converted into a new luxury home and apartments and given a new name.

Far Left: Reporters quiz the police outside Yew Tree Farm, on 20th September, 1978, the day after the body of Carl Bridgewater (left) was found.

Below, L–R: The Bridgewater Three, Michael Hickey, Vincent Hickey and James Robinson, walk free from the High Court in London on 29th July, 1997. The Hickeys had spent 18 years in jail before being cleared of the murder.

BIRMINGHAM
'RIVERS OF
BLOOD' SPEECH

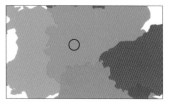

52° 28' 44" N, 1° 53' 52" W

20TH APRIL, 1968   BURLINGTON HOTEL (FORMERLY MIDLAND HOTEL), NEW STREET, BIRMINGHAM, B2 4JQ

WHERE ENOCH POWELL MADE HIS NOTORIOUS SPEECH ABOUT IMMIGRATION

Left: Midland Hotel, Birmingham, where Enoch Powell delivered his explosive speech on the immigration issue.

In a way it doesn't matter where one of the most explosive speeches in British political history was made. What matters is what was said and its impact. There's no doubt that Enoch Powell's so-called 'Rivers of Blood' speech would have been incendiary wherever it had been delivered. Nevertheless, there's something fascinating about going inside the hotel where the speech was made more than 40 years ago and feeling the reverberations.

Enoch Powell was an outspoken politician who was then the Conservative MP for Wolverhampton South-West. He delivered the speech to a Conservative Party

meeting at what was then the Midland Hotel near New Street Station in the centre of Birmingham, on the afternoon of Saturday, 20th April, 1968. This was three days before a bill was due to be debated in the House of Commons strengthening the law on racial discrimination.

ADVOCATING RACISM?

Powell never used the phrase "rivers of blood" in the speech. What he said was "As I look ahead, I am filled with foreboding, like the Roman, I seem to see the River Tiber foaming with much blood." The phrase came towards the end of a speech in which he spoke of the dangers, as he saw it, of the impact of immigration into Britain. Nevertheless, the speech became seen as a standard-bearer for opposition to immigration and was widely viewed as racist. The speech included calls for the repatriation of immigrants to their countries of origin and a rejection of the idea that immigrants and their descendants should be encouraged to maintain their own cultural traditions.

PUBLIC SUPPORT

According to those who were there, there was little negative reaction to the speech from the audience and a Gallup Poll conducted a few weeks later suggested that 74% of the British population thought Powell was right. However, the political and media reaction was immediate, with the majority condemning the speech. The following day Powell was sacked from the Shadow Cabinet by the Conservative leader, Edward Heath.

There's little doubt that Powell had intended to cause a furore. He had tipped off a journalist friend and ITV had an advance copy of the speech and, realising its significance, had sent a crew to film sections of it.

Thereafter Enoch Powell, who later left the Conservative Party, remained a hero to the far right (and less openly to many Conservatives), but a figure of hate for many until his death in 1998. The 'Rivers of Blood' speech has been repeatedly quoted in the years since it was delivered in a variety of political contexts.

The Midland Hotel became the Burlington Hotel in 1996 after a major refurbishment, but Powell's political time bomb still echoes down the years.

Above: Striding out near his London home in South Eaton Place, on 22nd April, 1968 is Enoch Powell, Conservative MP for Wolverhampton South-West, whose controversial speech on race relations in Birmingham led to his dismissal from Edward Heath's Shadow Cabinet.

BBC's
PEBBLE MILL

52° 27' 7" N, 1° 54' 47" W

1971–2004

PEBBLE MILL ROAD, EDGBASTON, BIRMINGHAM, B5 7SA

HOME OF 'PEBBLE MILL AT ONE' – FORMER HEADQUARTERS OF BBC MIDLANDS

Above: Without architectural merit, Pebble Mill was the nerve centre of BBC operations in the Midlands. The popular magazine magazine programme Pebble Mill at One was broadcast from the foyer and reception area.

Above: Rehearsals under way for the BBC's daytime TV show Pebble Mill at One, in the foyer of its Edgbaston headquarters.

Above: Sound recordists at work in the Pebble Mill car park, recording sound effects for the BBC Radio 4 soap The Archers.

Pebble Mill was the best-known BBC building outside London and it was all down to one programme. *Pebble Mill at One* was a lunchtime magazine show that ran first on BBC2 and then on BBC1 from 1972 to 1986, and was produced and presented from Birmingham. In the same vein as *Nationwide*, this folksy magazine show captured the imagination of television audiences and the rather gaunt building that hosted it basked in the reflected glory.

The building of Pebble Mill as an integrated headquarters for the BBC in the Midlands was an out-of-town development before such things became commonplace. It was opened by Princess Anne on 10th November, 1971 on a residential street in the upmarket Birmingham suburb of Edgbaston. Previously, the BBC's Birmingham operations had been based at Broad Street in the city centre and at a number of other studios. Pebble Mill was part of a BBC plan to bring its local, regional and network operations together in one building for each of its major centres outside London.

STUDIO SPACE

It was a large complex with seven storeys containing two TV studios, several radio studios and offices. It was home to a variety of network radio and TV programmes as well as the BBC's regional programmes for the Midlands, *Midlands Today* and the BBC's local radio station, BBC WM. The two most famous programmes made there were Radio 4 soap *The Archers* and *Pebble*

Mill at One. The latter was arguably the first purpose-made daytime TV show. It ran at lunchtime in an era when TV channels were not normally broadcasting throughout the day. It was broadcast from the foyer of the building. Its presenters included Bob Langley, Marion Foster, Donny Macleod and Jan Leeming. It was informal, appealingly chaotic at times a mixture of celebrity, consumer and entertainment content.

NEWS EMPHASIS

The programme was a victim of the changes introduced by John Birt in the late 1980s, including a stronger emphasis on news and current affairs. A new, extended lunchtime news was introduced on BBC1 and *Pebble Mill at One* was dropped, despite more than 30,000 viewers writing to the BBC to complain.

As the Millennium approached there were problems with both the lease and the structure. Also, changes in the technology of TV production meant that the BBC considered the building no longer fit for purpose. The corporation moved to a new centre at the Mailbox, back in the city centre, in October 2004.

The Pebble Mill site was bought by the then regional development agency, Advantage West Midlands, with plans to create a science and technology park. In 2005 Pebble Mill was demolished and for several years the site lay derelict. In late 2011 plans to build a new dental school and hospital were announced by the University of Birmingham as part of the redevelopment of the site.

COVENTRY'S
IRA BICYCLE BOMB

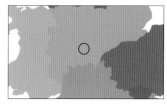

52° 24' 29" N, 1° 30' 38" W

25TH AUGUST, 1939   BROADGATE, COVENTRY, CV1 1LZ

AN IRA BOMB JUST A WEEK BEFORE THE SECOND WORLD WAR STARTED

Above: Surveying the damage. The crumpled remains of the bicycle used to deliver the devastating bomb can be seen alongside the car.

The IRA bombing campaign on mainland Britain is usually associated with the 1970s and beyond. However, there was a significant earlier campaign in the late 1930s in England, and Coventry was the scene of the most devastating attack just one week before German troops marched into Poland to begin the Second World War.

The attack on Coventry was part of the IRA's S-Plan, or Sabotage Plan, which had been under way since January 1939, when the organisation had declared war on Britain in pursuit of its objective of creating a united Ireland. From 16th January onward, bombs exploded at a series of targets around England.

At first, most of the targets were power stations and the infrastructure associated with water, gas and electricity. However, the targets also included more public places. In early February, two London underground stations were attacked, causing serious

injuries although no fatalities. Throughout the spring and summer the bombings continued in various towns and cities across the country, with railway stations becoming a particular target. There was widespread public alarm at the attacks, and the Government introduced tighter security measures and also passed legislation allowing the detention of foreigners.

CIVILIANS ATTACKED

Coventry was targeted on more than one occasion earlier in 1939, including a series of incendiary devices set off inside shops in the city, but no one was killed. However, by far the most serious incident in the IRA campaign occurred just after 2.30pm on a busy Friday afternoon, 25th August, in the heart of Coventry's shopping district. A bomb left in a bicycle carrier exploded outside Astley's in Broadgate. The bomb had been assembled at a house in Coventry and the bike had been parked on the kerb outside Astley's about half an hour before it exploded.

Five people died in the explosion, more than 100 were injured and over 40 premises were extensively damaged. Two people were convicted and subsequently hanged for their involvement in the bombing. Given that the aim of the IRA campaign was not to kill civilians, it has been speculated that the shopping centre was not the intended target and that, for some reason, the bicycle and its deadly cargo were abandoned there.

The centre of Coventry is much changed today, but the point where the explosion occurred is believed to be where the branch of Greggs the bakery chain now stands on Broadgate. The remains of the bicycle are kept in the Police Museum in Coventry.

Little more than a year after the IRA bombing, Coventry was subjected to one of the most devastating air-raids of the Second World War. An estimated 568 people died when the Luftwaffe attacked the city on 14th November, 1940, laying waste to large areas of the city centre, including the historic cathedral.

Above: Clearing up the debris. Severe damage was caused to property within the blast range of the 5lb explosive, which had an alarm clock as a timer.

CARDINGTON AIRSHIP
HANGARS

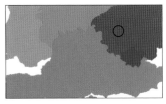

52° 6' 24" N, -0° 25' 45" E

4TH OCTOBER, 1930

RAF CARDINGTON, CARDINGTON, BEDFORDSHIRE, MK42 0UZ

THE DEPARTURE OF THE ILL-FATED
R101 AIRSHIP

Above: The airship R101 connected to the mooring mast at the Royal Airship Factory, Cardington, five days before its fateful maiden overseas voyage.

As you drive through the flat countryside not far from Bedford, two structures dominate the skyline. A pair of hangars stands tall among the otherwise featureless landscape. This is the place where one of the most romantic, yet ultimately tragic, episodes in transport history was played out.

The Royal Airship Factory, later the Royal Airship Works, at Cardington, started its life as an aviation centre in 1915 when Short Brothers established a base there to build military airships under a contract with the Admiralty. An area of farmland was already being used as an aerodrome by the Royal Flying Corps. Shorts chose the site because it was near to Bedford, which was well-blessed with light engineering firms and because the prevailing winds were moderate.

The first airship project lasted from 1915 until 1921.

Above: Miss Ellen Wilkinson, Labour MP, prepares to board the R101 airship at Cardington.

The objective was to build airships to rival the German Zeppelins. In fact, the first airship built at Cardington was only commissioned five days before the end of the First World War. The project continued, but was cancelled in 1921 and Cardington was closed.

ASSEMBLY SHEDS

However, Cardington got a second, and ultimately better-known, lease of life in 1924, when Imperial Airways announced a project to build civilian airships. Cardington's hangar was enlarged to facilitate this project, and a second hangar was taken down at RNAS Pulham in Norfolk and reconstructed at Cardington.

The dimensions were breathtaking. The hangars were 812 feet long, 272 feet wide and 180 feet high. The floor area was equal to 16 Olympic swimming pools, and Nelson's Column would not reach the top. A mast, more than 196 feet high, also had to be built to moor the airships.

The result of this project was the R101, effectively a Government-funded project designed to deliver a civilian airship capable of flying long distances throughout the British Empire. After a long development period and many modifications, the R101 took off amid a great fanfare from Cardington on the early evening of

Above: The giant nose piece of the R101 rigid airship under construction at Cardington using stainless-steel girders made by Norwich-based aircraft manufacturer Boulton and Paul.

Above: Girders forming the tailpiece of the R101 are bolted together in one of the two hangars at the Royal Airship Works.

4th October, 1930, heading for Karachi, Pakistan. It was never to get there. The airship crashed in a field near Beauvais, not far from Paris, the following day, killing 48 of the 54 people on board, including the Secretary of State for Air, Lord Thomson.

The R101 crash marked the end of the airships programme. However, Cardington was converted to a new use in the run-up to, and during the Second World War. In 1936 it started making barrage balloons and it became the RAF Balloon Training Unit and also a meteorological station.

Since the war, the Cardington site has been put to many uses, including as a training centre for driving examiners and as a fire research station. There was a brief flirtation with airships in the 1980s and more recently by a company based at Cardington trying to develop a new style of airship, the Skycat and its prototype, the Skykitten.

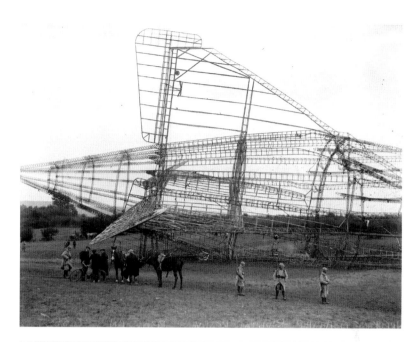

In early 2012, one of the hangars was used by the film industry. Among films shot at Cardington are *Dark Knight*, *Batman Begins* and *Inception*. The hangar has also been used for music videos and rehearsals by bands. Longer-term plans for the other hangar were still uncertain.

Nevertheless, the two hangars still loom over the Bedfordshire countryside as a monument to a bygone age of travel.

Main picture: Monumental pair. Shed 1 (left) is 812 feet long, 272 feet wide and 180 feet high. The floor area is 5 acres and the total volume of the building is 26,840,000 cubic feet.

Top: The mangled wreckage of the R101 lies in a field in Beauvais, France, on 5th October, 1930 after its tragic crash

Above: One of Goodyear's modern fleet of non-rigid, polyester airships, known as 'blimps', inside one of the Cardington hangars in 2002.

CLIVEDEN
HOUSE

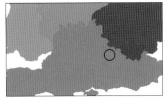

51° 33' 29" N, -0° 41' 17" E

CLIVEDEN HOUSE, TAPLOW, BERKSHIRE, SL6 0JF

THE SETTING FOR THE PROFUMO AFFAIR

Above: Cliveden, the Italianate mansion and estate at Taplow, Berkshire, pictured on 28th September, 1939. Set on the banks 130 feet above the River Thames, its grounds slope down to the river. The site has been home to an earl, two dukes, a Prince of Wales and the Viscounts Astor.

Above: Pictured at their Cliveden estate on 1st September, 1920 , is Waldorf Astor, the 2nd Viscount Astor, and his wife Nancy, Viscountess Astor, the first woman to serve as a member of Parliament in Great Britain, in 1919.

Stately homes have not otherwise featured on this journey, but Cliveden has a special place in 20th-century British history. It was the scene of a political scandal that rocked the nation in the 1960s, and contributed to the resignation of a prime minister and the defeat of a government at a subsequent general election.

Cliveden's history stretches back to 1666 when the first house was built on the site. It was destroyed by fire as was its replacement. The current house was built by Charles Barry in 1851. In 1893 Cliveden was bought by the Astors, an Anglo-American family of German descent, and throughout the 1920s and 1930s it became a major location on the social circuit.

The beauty of the house and its surroundings on the banks of the Thames, plus its proximity to London, made an invitation to Cliveden something that famous and wealthy people found hard to resist. Charlie Chaplin, Winston Churchill, George Bernard Shaw, Rudyard Kipling and T.E. Lawrence (of Arabia) were among those who stayed there. During the 1930s the house also became associated with the

Above: War Minister John Profumo resigned from the Government on 5th June, 1963, after his affair with Christine Keeler was revealed.

Above: Christine Keeler, the model and showgirl who was at the centre of the Profumo affair that rocked the Convservative Government.

Above: Yevgeny Ivanov, a naval attaché at the Soviet Embassy in London, had an affair with Keeler while she was also involved with Profumo.

so-called 'Cliveden Set', a group of Anglo-American right-wing intellectuals who were thought to be at the forefront of the policy of appeasement of Hitler. They were often portrayed later as pro-Nazi, although historians disagree about how justified this description was. In 1942 the Astors gave Cliveden to the National Trust on condition they could remain there until their deaths.

CHANCE MEETING

It was during the post-war period that Cliveden's most famous episode occurred. In July 1961 Cliveden's resident osteopath, Dr Stephen Ward, was hosting a house party at his home, Spring Cottage. His guests included model and showgirl Christine Keeler and Yevgeny Ivanov, a naval attaché at the Soviet Embassy in London.

When Ward took his friends to the pool at the main house, they were met by 3rd Viscount William Astor and his guests, who included John Profumo, the then Secretary of State for War in Harold Macmillan's Conservative Government, and his actress wife Valerie Hobson.

After this chance meeting with Keeler, Profumo embarked upon a short affair with her, unaware that she was also in a relationship with Ivanov. At the time relations between the West and the Soviet Union were tense. The Cold War was at its height, so any relationship between a government minister and someone associated with the Soviet Union was potentially highly damaging to Britain's national security.

For more than a year the affair remained a secret, even though the press were aware of rumours. It only came out into the open after Keeler failed to turn up in court as a witness in a criminal case involving a former lover. Her absence fuelled media speculation, and in March 1963 a Labour MP used parliamentary privilege to raise the matter in the House of Commons, claiming that national security had been put at risk.

"NO IMPROPRIETY"

When the scandal first broke, Profumo admitted that he knew Keeler, but denied any impropriety in their relationship. However, newspaper stories then appeared about the affair and Profumo had to admit that he had lied to the House of Commons about

Above: The elegant façade of the Cliveden Hotel, viewed from the parterre, on 10th June, 2005.

the nature of the relationship with Keeler, and he resigned in June 1963.

There was never any evidence that any secrets had been passed to the Russians as a result of the affair. However, the scandal contributed to the sense of decline and decay in the Macmillan Government. Macmillan resigned a few months later and the Conservatives, under Sir Alec Douglas Home, lost the 1964 General Election.

Profumo's wife stood by him. After his resignation, Profumo never spoke publicly about the affair. He devoted himself to charity work in the East End of London for which he later received a CBE. He was largely seen as having rehabilitated himself and having restored his reputation by the time of his death in 2006.

Cliveden remains in the ownership of the National Trust, but the house is now run commercially as a luxury spa hotel. The hotel makes something of the association with the Profumo Affair in its promotion. The swimming pool and Spring Cottage where the famous guests frolicked back in 1961 are still there. The hotel's rather fitting motto is "Nothing ordinary ever happened here, nor could it."

ALDERMASTON
MARCH

51° 21' 48" N, 1° 8' 28" W

4TH APRIL, 1958   ATOMIC WEAPONS ESTABLISHMENT, ALDERMASTON, BERKSHIRE, RG7 4PR

FOCUS OF THE ANTI-NUCLEAR PROTESTS
OF THE 1950s ONWARD

Above: The Australian and Swedish contingents in the anti-H bomb march from the Atomic Weapons Research Establishment at Aldermaston, Berkshire, to London, on 27th March, 1959.

On Good Friday 1958 several thousand people marched from Trafalgar Square in London and arrived on Easter Monday at the Atomic Weapons Research Establishment (AWRE), which had been established on the site of RAF Aldermaston in Berkshire. They were protesting against the build up of nuclear weapons being undertaken by Britain and other countries as the Cold War between the West and the Soviet bloc intensified.

Since then the name 'Aldermaston' has become synonymous with CND, the Campaign for Nuclear Disarmament, which started in the 1950s in protest at the proliferation of nuclear weapons. In fact the first Aldermaston march was organised by the Direct Action Committee Against Nuclear War, although endorsed by the newly formed CND.

CND CAMPAIGNERS

In popular memory, the Aldermaston Marches are seen as a regular feature of political life for many years thereafter. In fact, they were only held annually from 1959 to 1963, but during those years, the marches were a central focus of the CND campaign. CND, which took them over, reversed the direction of the 52-mile walk so that they started at Aldermaston, but ended at the seat of government power in London. The numbers taking part grew to an estimated 150,000 and the 1963 march ended with some violent clashes with police. Thereafter the marches have not been held annually, but have been revived on a number of occasions, including a mass event on the 50th anniversary in 2008.

The AWRE had been established in the early 1950s. The RAF base had been opened in 1942 and was used by both British and American personnel during the remainder of the war. After the war Aldermaston was originally intended to be a flying school, but was designated a temporary civilian airport and was apparently even considered as a possible site for London's third airport. However, in 1950, with the Cold War intensifying, it was selected to be the main base for the development and research of nuclear weapons.

WARHEAD MANUFACTURE

The management of AWRE was privatised in the early 1990s and is now known as AWE, being run by a consortium of private companies, although the Government retains a 'golden share' and owns the site. The Cold War may be over, but Britain remains a nuclear power and Aldermaston remains the main site for the development and manufacture of warheads for Britain's nuclear deterrent. Aldermaston is currently undergoing a major refurbishment, which anti-nuclear campaigners have described as an expansion. Although the Aldermaston marches no longer take place on a regular basis, there is a monthly protest by women's peace groups outside the plant.

Above: Labour MP Michael Foot (L) was among campaigners against nuclear armaments on a march from Aldermaston to Trafalgar Square, London, on 15th April, 1960.

Above: Centre of attention. The Atomic Research Establishment at Aldermaston, pictured on 21st March, 2012.

HESTON
AERODROME

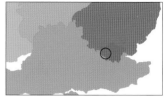

51° 29' 8" N, -0° 23' 52" E

30TH SEPTEMBER, 1938

AERODROME WAY, HESTON, LONDON, TW5 9QB

SCENE OF A FAMOUS SPEECH AND NEARLY ONE OF LONDON'S MAJOR AIRPORTS

Above: British Prime Minister Neville Chamberlain makes his famous 'Peace in our time' speech upon returning from talks with German Chancellor Adolf Hitler in Munich, on 30th September, 1938.

Heston Aerodrome has two particular claims to fame and both provoke the thought of what might have been. It is best known as the place to which the then British Prime Minister, Neville Chamberlain, returned after a series of meetings with Adolf Hitler, in September 1938, to declare that the Munich Agreement meant "Peace in our time". It is also the place that had been intended, and might have become, one of London's main airports.

The story of Heston Aerodrome is part of the romance of the developing business of civilian air travel between the two world wars. Alongside Croydon, Le Touquet, Templehof and many others long since departed, Heston was one of the pioneering locations of air travel. It was opened in 1929 – the brainchild of two pilots, Nigel Norman and Alan Muntz. At first it was used for flying schools, air displays, private flying and as a base for air shows and long-distance record attempts.

AIR TRAVEL BOOM

However, as the possibilities of expanding commercial air travel opened up in the 1930s, Heston developed. In 1931 it was renamed Heston Airport and facilities for passengers were built. Regular services started to the Isle of Wight, to Jersey, to Le Touquet and to Blackpool. Croydon Airport, to the south of London, was seen as the leading airport, but Heston was a significant player in the developing air travel business.

During the late 1930s the Government investigated how aviation could be developed and its plan for growing airport capacity around London involved four sites – developing the existing airports at Croydon and Heston as well as building new airports at Fairlop in Essex and Lullingstone in Kent. Heston was bought by the Air Ministry and work began to develop it into what would have been London's second airport alongside Croydon. New lighting and drainage were installed, the runway improved and land was bought to allow expansion.

As this expansion was starting to take effect, Heston's most famous hour took place. In September 1938 Neville Chamberlain flew from Heston on three occasions in as many weeks to meet the German Chancellor, Adolf Hitler. Apart from the political significance of these trips, the method of transport was significant because, at the time, it was novel for politicians to travel by air.

WAR AND PEACE

Chamberlain returned to a hero's welcome at Heston, after the third meeting, with the Munich Agreement, which he believed would avoid a war between Britain and Germany. On Friday, 30th September he stepped off the plane at Heston waving his agreement with Hitler to cheering crowds and making a short speech, although his most famous line, "Peace in our time", was actually uttered later in Downing Street.

But it was the failure of Chamberlain's policy of appeasement that helped to trigger Heston's demise. When war was declared in 1939, the airport expansion plans for London were abandoned. In the early part of the war, Heston did continue with some civilian flights, but it was mainly used for military purposes from 1940 onward. Spitfires and Hurricanes were among the planes that flew from Heston during the war.

At the end of the war it was decided to develop Heathrow as London's main airport, and later Gatwick became the second. Heston closed in 1947. It wasn't until 1978 that the last connection with aviation ended, when the Civil Aviation Authority moved out of the aerodrome buildings that it had used as offices. The site where the aerodrome stood is now a golf course and an industrial estate. One hangar still exists and is a Grade-2 listed building. The M4 motorway cuts through the site and the Heston service station is built on part of what was once the airfield. The main road from the days of the airfield, Aerodrome Way, still exists and a number of other roads on the site also bear aviation-related names.

Heston's sister airport of Croydon suffered a similar demise after the war, and the two proposed new airports at Fairlop and Lullingstone were never built.

Above: Links to Heston's involvement with aviation are still in evidence.

SITE OF THE
FESTIVAL OF BRITAIN

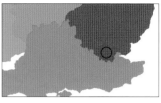

51° 30' 20" N, -0° 7' 0" E

3RD MAY–30TH SEPTEMBER, 1951   SOUTH BANK CENTRE, BELVEDERE ROAD, LONDON SE1 8XX

BRITAIN'S TONIC FOR POST-WAR AUSTERITY

What happened on what is now the South Bank in central London in 1951 is part of a continuum stretching right back to the Great Exhibition of 1851 and continuing through to the Millennium Dome. The urge to create great public exhibitions and festivals as an act of national pride was really a creation of the 19th century. However, it is a tendency that continued right through the 20th and into the 21st centuries. The legacy left behind at the places where such festivals took place is a fascinating one.

The notion of a major celebration in 1951 was first conceived well before the Second World War was over, and the original idea was for an international fair to commemorate the centenary of the Great Exhibition. However, in 1945, as the war ended, the Government appointed a committee to consider the idea and the notion of an international fair was abandoned on grounds of cost.

POST-WAR REGENERATION

Instead, the idea of a Festival of Britain was decided upon, described by the event's director, Gerald Barry, as "a tonic to the nation" that would generate a feeling of progress and regeneration in the aftermath of the war. The Festival would celebrate Britain's contribution to the arts, science, technology and engineering, and would be a statement of confidence about the nation's future. The other main objective was to provide a showcase for new ideas about design that could influence the rebuilding of London and other British towns and cities.

The main focus of the Festival of Britain was on a site on the south bank of the Thames in the Waterloo area of London. Previously, the area had been occupied by warehouses, railway sidings and housing, and it had suffered considerable bomb damage.

Right: The Festival of Britain emblem – the Festival Star – designed by Abram Games, was featured on the cover of the South Bank Exhibition Guide, 1951.

Facing page: An aerial photograph of the Festival of Britain's main site shows the Dome of Discovery (C) and the Skylon to its right, with the Royal Festival Hall (foreground R), the only building to survive to the present day. The Houses of Parliament are seen on the opposite bank.

Above: The cigar-shaped steel tensegrity structure, Skylon, and the Dome of Discovery on the South Bank of the River Thames, viewed from Victoria Embankment. A popular joke of the time was that, like the British economy of 1951, the Skylon "...had no visible means of support".

Above: Dominated by the Dome of Discovery, long queues form for admission into the festival exhibitions.

Above right: The view towards Rodney Pier (background) with a Sport pavilion adjacent, the Harbour Bar (R) and the base of the Shot Tower just visible (L).

Right: The Land of Britain Pavilion (foreground, R) by H.T. Cadbury-Brown RA, one of two cone-shaped entrance structures that flanked one of the main viewpoints. At night, visitors looked across a light-studded pavement towards the river, where a bank of fountains was lit by gas jets, and red globe lights were festooned in the trees. The Transport Pavilion (background) featured gliders and the Schneider Trophy winning Supermarine S6B seaplane.

PRIZE EXHIBITS

Perhaps the best remembered features of the Festival site were the Dome of Discovery and the Skylon Tower. The Dome, the largest such structure in the world at the time, was 93 feet high and 365 feet in diameter. It contained exhibitions about British initiatives in exploration and discovery, including the land, the sea, polar, space and others. The Skylon Tower was a thin steel and aluminium tower pointing 300 feet into the air, which was lit from within at night and which became the defining symbol of the Festival.

Other features of the site included the Royal Festival Hall and a temporary cinema, the Telekinema, which showcased film and the then new medium of television. The only pre-existing building to be incorporated into the

Festival site was the Shot Tower from the former Lambeth Lead Works, which was turned into a radio beacon.

The Festival was neither confined to the South Bank nor just to London. Elsewhere in the capital, the Festival Pleasure Gardens were created in Battersea Park. A new wing was opened at the Science Museum in South Kensington, where a science exhibition was put on for the festival. A new housing development was built at the Lansbury Estate in Poplar as a design showcase.

There were exhibitions and festivals in a number of cities and towns around the country, and an exhibition on board the ship HMS *Campania*, which toured the coastline of Britain.

The cost of the festival was around £8m (about £200m at 2012 prices). There was criticism about the cost at a time when the country was still recovering from the war and many cities and towns were still wrecked by bomb damage. However, it proved immensely popular and more than eight million people visited the South Bank site. A similar number visited the Festival Pleasure Gardens, and 900,000 people visited the festival ship when it docked around the country.

SITE DEVELOPMENT

Nevertheless, the Festival of Britain became a party political issue. The Labour Government of Clement Attlee elected in 1945 had initiated the festival and enthusiastically championed it. Political leadership of the festival was in the hands of the Deputy Prime Minister, Herbert Morrison, and he and Attlee believed that a successful event would help Labour retain power in the 1951 General Election. However, Labour lost the election. The incoming Conservative Government, led by Winston Churchill, saw the festival as political propaganda by the Labour Government and ordered the removal of the festival buildings.

The only structure that survived permanently, and which was always intended to do so, was the Royal Festival Hall. The Telekinema survived temporarily until it was replaced by a new National Film Theatre. The site of the Dome of Discovery is now the Jubilee Gardens between Hungerford Bridge and County Hall. The Skylon stood on the riverbank not far from where the London Eye now stands. The Dome and the Skylon were sold for scrap.

Although the Festival site stood empty for many years after 1951, nearly all of it has progressively been redeveloped for various cultural and entertainment uses, including the Queen Elizabeth Hall, the Purcell Room, the Hayward Gallery and what is now the BFI Southbank, formerly the National Film Theatre. In addition, the National Theatre was built adjacent to the site.

The Festival of Britain site, like the White City site in London before it and the Millennium Dome later, has found a new public use after its initial temporary function had been fulfilled.

Right: The Festival of Britain showcased the best of British goods, as revealed in this catalogue produced by The Council of Industrial Design.

Above: An aerial photograph of Battersea Park, Wandsworth, which hosted the Festival Pleasure Gardens.

WINDRUSH ARRIVAL
TILBURY
DOCKS

51° 27' 4" N, 0° 21' 51" E

22ND JUNE, 1948

FERRY ROAD, TILBURY, ESSEX, RM18 7NG

WHERE POST-WAR IMMIGRATION INTO BRITAIN BEGAN

On Tuesday, 22nd June, 1948 almost 500 people from the West Indies stepped off a ship in bright sunshine at Tilbury Docks in Essex to begin a new life in Britain. However, their arrival into the post-war austerity of the late 1940s marked not just a new beginning for them, but also a new era that would create a multi-cultural society in Britain over the following 50 years and more.

Immigration into Britain didn't start in 1948. People had come here from all sorts of places before. But the arrival of the HMT *Empire Windrush* did mark something special and different in that it was the result of a deliberate government initiative to try to deal with shortages in the labour market in post-war Britain. An advertisement had appeared in a newspaper in Jamaica offering cheap passage to Britain (£28 in 1948 prices – equivalent to approximately £800 in 2012).

FOUNDING COMMUNITIES

Most of those who came on the *Windrush* were housed at first in the deep shelter at Clapham South Underground Station. It was for this reason that the surrounding area, notably Brixton, became a focal point for African-Caribbean immigrants from the 1950s. Many of the *Windrush* group only intended to stay for a while, but in the end, most settled permanently. Their story, and that of other immigrants to Britain, from the Caribbean, from the Indian sub-continent and elsewhere, was to be a mixed one. For many, acceptance by the indigenous population was a slow and painful process, marked by racism and discrimination. Throughout the second half of the 20th century and into the 21st century, the issue of immigration into Britain remained politically controversial.

ILLUSTRIOUS CAREER

The *Windrush* itself had a fascinating history both before and after its most famous moment. It had been launched in Hamburg in December 1930. Before the Second World War, it had been a cruise ship bearing the name *Monte Rosa*. Among other assignments during the 1930s, it played a role in the Nazi Party's 'Strength through Joy' programme. Loyal members of the Nazi Party were rewarded with cruises on the ship.

During the Second World War it became part of the German war effort as a troop carrier, but also as a transport ship taking Norwegian Jews to concentration camps, and in 1945 to rescue Germans trapped in East Prussia by the advance of the Russians as the war ended.

In 1945 the ship was taken by the British Government as a war prize and converted into a transport ship for use by the Ministry of Transport. It was renamed HMT *Empire Windrush* in 1947 and used to ferry British troops around the world, including to the Korean War. It was bringing back wounded soldiers and others from the Korean War in February 1954, on what proved to be its last voyage. Plagued by engine failures and other problems, when it sailed from Port Said, its engine room caught fire. Four crew died, but all 1,200 passengers survived. The burned-out hulk of the ship was towed towards Gibraltar, but sank on 30th March, 1954.

In 1998, to mark the 50th anniversary of the arrival of the *Windrush*, a square in Brixton was renamed Windrush Square. Ten years later, a plaque was unveiled at the London Cruise Terminal at Tilbury Docks near where the ship had docked back in 1948.

Tilbury Docks remains a thriving port. The *Windrush* is no more, but those who arrived on board in 1948, and successive generations of their families, have become an integral part of British society.

Above: Jamaican immigrants are welcomed by RAF officials from the Colonial Office after the ex-troopship HMT Empire Windrush *(facing page) landed them at Tilbury docks.*

FINSBURY PARK
ASTORIA

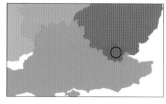

31ST MARCH, 1967   232 SEVEN SISTERS ROAD, FINSBURY PARK, LONDON, N4 3NX

WHERE JIMI HENDRIX SET FIRE TO HIS GUITAR

Far Left: The charismatic Jimi Hendrix performing live on stage in 1969.
Left: Scorched. Hendrix's 1965 Fender Stratocaster, the first guitar he burnt on stage, displayed on 24th July, 2008, was sold for £280,000 in September 2008.

As you come into King's Cross Station, London, on the East Coast mainline, you see a building to the right, at a junction on the Seven Sisters Road, that was clearly a cinema and that, on closer inspection, can now be seen to be the Universal Church of the Kingdom of God. Like many former cinemas all over the country, it has found a new use. However, in between showing films and worshipping God, the Finsbury Park Astoria had a life as a live music venue.

It was during this phase of its existence that the Astoria witnessed one of those celebrated moments in the history of popular music that has become legendary. Almost certainly the number of people who claim to have been there on the night Jimi Hendrix set fire to his guitar far exceeds the capacity of the Finsbury Park Astoria, but it's a great story and

people can be forgiven for wanting to be associated with it.

The Astoria was opened on 29th September, 1930 – one of four Astorias built in London at the time. It was ornate with a Moorish style foyer, a theatre organ and a capacity of almost 3,500. In the 1960s, although it was still operating as a cinema, it staged one-off concerts on its large stage. It was during this period that Jimi Hendrix appeared there.

FLAMING FINALE

It was 31st March, 1967 the first night of the Walker Brothers tour. Cat Stevens and Jimi Hendrix were the support artists, with Englebert Humperdinck as special guest star. During his act, Hendrix used a cigarette

lighter to set fire to his Fender Stratocaster guitar. His fingers were burnt and he needed hospital treatment, although the guitar was only scorched. Hendrix's motives in setting fire to the guitar remain unclear, but he later repeated the stunt in Miami and it was copied by others.

Meanwhile, the Astoria, which had been renamed as the Odeon, closed as a cinema in 1971 and reopened as the Rainbow Theatre. For the next 11 years it was a leading London music venue. Among the bands who performed there were The Who, Pink Floyd, Genesis, Bob Marley and the Wailers, Van Morrison and Thin Lizzy.

In 1982 the Rainbow was closed and was largely unused for 13 years, until it was bought by the Universal Church of the Kingdom of God – a Brazilian Pentecostal church, which made it their UK headquarters.

Above: The Finsbury Park Astoria after it had shut as the Rainbow in 1982.
Right: An advertisement for the forthcoming concert at the Astoria, which featured Jimi Hendrix as a support act for the Walker Brothers, on the occasion he burnt his Fender Stratocaster.

PICKLES
AND THE WORLD CUP

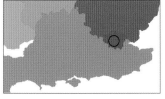

51° 24' 59" N, -0° 5' 48" E

27TH MARCH, 1966

BEULAH HILL, NORWOOD, LONDON, SE19

STOLEN WORLD CUP FOUND BY A DOG IN A SUBURBAN GARDEN

Left: Pickles with his owner David Corbett at the spot where the trophy was discovered in the Corbetts' garden.

Above: Jubilant England captain Bobby Moore raises the Jules Rimet Trophy as he is chaired by other members of the victorious team.

Above: David Corbett and Pickles celebrate their good fortune while watching the 1966 World Cup Final on television.

"The body was discovered by a man walking his dog" is a familiar refrain in the language of journalism. Less common is "The World Cup was discovered by a man out walking his dog". However, that is precisely what happened on Sunday, 27th March, 1966, in the South London suburb of Norwood. David Corbett's dog Pickles discovered a package in the garden of their home in Beulah Hill. On closer examination, Corbett realised that his trusty mongrel had found the Jules Rimet Trophy, the football World Cup, which was due to be competed for later that year in England.

The trophy had gone missing a week earlier from the Methodist Central Hall in London, where it had been on display as part of a postage-stamp exhibition. Despite the security precautions, it had been removed from the exhibition. A massive police operation was launched to find it and spare the embarrassment of the English footballing authorities, who were hosting the sport's most prestigious competition for the first time.

A £15,000 ransom demand was received by the then chairman of the Football Association, Joe Mears.

A rendezvous was fixed for an exchange with a man called Edward Bletchley. Mears tipped off the police, but Bletchley became suspicious and fled. He was later caught and charged and served two years in prison.

Various conspiracy theories persist about what really happened. Initially Pickles' owner was suspected of involvement by the police. Some still believe the whole thing was a publicity stunt. Nevertheless, Pickles became a national hero. England won the World Cup. Pickles and his owner were invited to the celebratory banquet. Sadly, Pickles was only able to enjoy his celebrity status for a short while. He was choked to death by his own lead while chasing a cat in 1967.

Joe Mears died in June 1966 and never saw England win the World Cup. Edward Bletchley died of emphysema shortly after his release from prison. The Jules Rimet Trophy was also not to survive for long. After Brazil won the competition for the third time in 1970, they were allowed to keep it. In 1983 it was stolen from a secure cabinet in Rio de Janeiro and melted down. The thieves were never caught and a new trophy was made for subsequent World Cups.

DEATH
AT EPSOM RACECOURSE

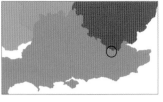

51° 18' 47" N, -0° 15' 11" E

4TH JUNE, 1913

TATTENHAM CORNER, EPSOM RACECOURSE, EPSOM DOWNS, SURREY, KT18 5LQ

MOST DRAMATIC SUFFRAGETTE PROTEST

Above: An unconscious Emily Davison lies beneath Anmer with a fractured skull. Jockey Herbert Jones was haunted by her face for many years.

It was one of the most remarkable acts of political protest in history – a woman throwing herself in front of the King's horse at one of the leading events on the racing and social calendar to advance the cause of female suffrage. It has acquired such iconic status perhaps partly because it was captured on film and by press photographers.

It was Derby Day at Epsom – Wednesday, 4th June, 1913 – and the King's horse, Anmer, was running. Davison stepped out in front of the horse on the bend at Tattenham Corner, causing the animal to fall. She was knocked to the ground unconscious and suffered serious injuries from which she died four days later. Her funeral took place in London, but she is buried in the grounds of St Mary the Virgin in Morpeth, Northumberland, near where she had lived with her mother.

PREVIOUS OFFENCES

This was the most dramatic, but not the first of Davison's violent acts in pursuit of the suffragette cause. Born in 1872, she had previously been a school governess and a teacher, and had studied at Oxford and London universities. In 1906 she joined the Women's Social and Political Union (WSPU) and in 1908 gave up teaching to devote herself full-time to the cause. She was arrested and imprisoned several times for a variety of acts, including the bombing of Lloyd George's house.

MOTIVE DOUBTS

Almost a century after the incident, arguments continue about her true motives on the day of the Derby. She had a return ticket to London in her possession, which has led many people to believe that she didn't intend to take her own life. It is speculated that she simply wanted to attach a WSPU flag to the King's horse.

In addition, there is still dispute about the significance of her actions that day at Epsom. Some claim that her dramatic, ultimately fatal gesture advanced the cause of votes for women, but others claim that she set the cause back because of the popularity of the monarchy. Women's suffrage was achieved a few years later, after the First World War, although at first only for women over 30 and with minimum property qualifications. It wasn't until 1928 that universal women's suffrage was achieved in Britain.

The plan of Epsom Racecourse still follows a similar layout as it did a hundred years ago and the bend at Tattenham Corner, where the fateful protest took place, is still there. There is no plaque or memorial commemorating the event at the racecourse. However, in early 2012, the racecourse was discussing how to mark the centenary in 2013. Away from the course, a nearby road is named Emily Davison Drive. There are plaques commemorating Davison in the House of Commons and at the former Epsom and Ewell Cottage Hospital.

Above: Jockey Herbert Jones is carried away on a stretcher. He suffered mild concussion and a broken rib after being thrown from Anmer.

Above: Emily Davison's funeral procession passes through Piccadilly Circus in London. Was her death deliberate or a tragic accident?

BROOKLANDS
RACING CIRCUIT

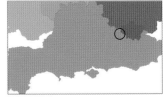

51° 21' 8" N, -0° 27' 33" E

7TH AUGUST, 1926

BROOKLANDS ROAD, WEYBRIDGE, SURREY, KT13 0QN

BIRTHPLACE OF BRITISH MOTOR RACING

Above: The start of the Junior Car Club 200-mile race at Brooklands on 26th September, 1925. The race was won by Henry Segrave in a Darracq.

Above: Kaye Don's massive Sunbeam Silver Bullet at Brooklands. The huge car, built with the aim of raising the land speed record in 1929, was powered by a pair of supercharged 24-litre aero engines, but it failed to achieve any records.

I t's surely not just petrolheads or plane enthusiasts who can identify with the romance associated with Brooklands. Hidden amid the prosperous commuter belt of Surrey is a venue that truly deserves the label 'iconic'. The very name Brooklands conjures up the smell and sounds of cars and aeroplanes, and positively reeks of the 1920s and 1930s. Although the place is probably most associated with motor racing, the site has also made an enormous contribution to the history of aviation and aircraft production.

The Brooklands Motor circuit opened on 17th June, 1907 and was the first purpose-built motor-racing circuit in the world. It was created by a local landowner Hugh Locke King on his estate. The original motivation was to have somewhere to test cars at high speeds. With the advent of the motor car around the turn of the 20th century, a speed limit of 20mph was introduced on all Britain's roads. So somewhere was needed for the growing car industry to test their products.

RECORD BREAKERS

The appeal of racing cars as a spectator sport grew quickly. The original track was an oval shape – two and three-quarter miles in length – with an additional finishing straight. Probably its most distinctive features were the steeply-banked bends at each end of the track. In the period from its opening in 1907 to the First World War in 1914, Brooklands played host to a wide variety of motor-racing events for both cars and motorbikes, and a number of records were set and broken.

Within a few days of being opened, Brooklands was the scene of a world record. Motor-racing pioneer Selwyn Francis Edge completed 1,581 miles in 24 hours of continuous driving at an average of 66 miles per hour to establish a record that stood for 17 years. In 1913 Percy Lambert achieved a record speed of over 103 miles per hour, but was killed at the track a few months later trying to better his own record.

Alongside the development of motor racing, Brooklands played an important role in aviation history. The aerodrome opened in 1908 and was the scene of the first flight trials of British powered aircraft. A number of flying schools were based at Brooklands, including the Sopwith Flying School, opened by Thomas Sopwith in 1912.

During the First World War, motor racing stopped. The site was requisitioned for the war effort and became a centre for the building and testing of military aircraft. Sopwith had started assembling aeroplanes on the site in 1912 and Vickers established a factory there in the old Itala car works in 1915. After the First World War, Brooklands' role in aviation continued, with Vickers and Hawker building thousands of aircraft. The aerodrome was the base for flying schools and was used by the RAF for training pilots during the late 1930s.

Throughout the 1920s and 1930s, cars and planes co-existed during what was the heyday of Brooklands. After repairs to the racing circuit, which had been damaged in the war, grand prix racing came to the Surrey circuit.

It was the brainchild of Henry Segrave, who had taken part in, and won, the French and San Sebastian grands prix in 1923. The first British Grand Prix took place at Brooklands on Saturday, 7th August, 1926 and was won by the Frenchmen Louis Wagner and Robert Senechal sharing the driving in a Delage 15 S8. They beat Briton Malcolm Campbell in a Bugatti. The event was repeated at Brooklands the following year.

During the 1920s and 1930s, Brooklands was the home of British motor racing, with a whole host of different events there. It remained the only major motor-racing circuit in Britain until Donington opened in 1931, and it became part of the society circuit alongside the Henley Regatta and Wimbledon. Facilities were improved and in 1937 a new road-style circuit was added, designed by Malcolm Campbell. However, the British Grand Prix was never held there again. After the initial two years, the event lapsed until after the Second World War, although two Donington grands prix were held at that circuit in 1937 and 1938.

CIRCUIT CLOSURE

The effective end of the Brooklands circuit came with the outbreak of the Second World War. The last race meeting to be held at Brooklands was on 7th August, 1939. The site was once again used for wartime aircraft production. Wellingtons, Warwicks and Hurricanes were the principal

Above: Rows of de Havilland Moth biplanes lined up in front of the Brooklands Aviation School of Flying in September 1933.

Above: The amenities at Brooklands were not always restricted to cars and aeroplanes, as this photo of a cycle race in June 1933 demonstrates.

Above: Well-known Brooklands motorcycle racer Bert Denly at speed on the banking on a 500cc Norton 18 in May 1928.

Above: Autocar sports editor and successful racer Sammy Davis pilots his Bentley around one of the Brooklands banked turns in July 1929.

planes made there. Parts of the track were damaged and other parts were sacrificed for the needs of aircraft production, with hangars and access roads built on them. Trees were planted on some sections of the circuit as part of the camouflaging of the Vickers factory. Nevertheless, the factory suffered a direct hit in an air-raid in September 1940, which killed 88 aircraft workers, injured more than 400 and caused extensive damage. After the end of the war, the whole site, including the much damaged circuit, was sold to Vickers-Armstrong and aircraft production continued there until the late 1980s.

Today, about half of the original circuit, including most of the banking, remains and Brooklands' dual role in both motoring and aviation history is commemorated in the Brooklands Museum, which opened in 1987. Mercedes-Benz World, which includes vehicle test tracks and offers a range of off-road driving experiences, opened on part of the site in 2006. Parts of the rest of the site are now given over to a variety of businesses, shops and housing. The remains of the banked circuit are used by both the museum and Mercedes-Benz World for a range of motoring purposes.

Brooklands' glory days were recaptured in novel fashion in 2009 when BBC presenter James May and a team of volunteers recreated the track in Scalextric for a programme broadcast in November of that year.

Above: Brooklands monument and preserved flight booking office. Built in 1911, the latter is thought to be the world's first flight booking office.

Above: A section of the original banked track that can still be seen on the Brooklands site. Occasionally it is used for commemorative events.

FARNBOROUGH
BALLOON
SCHOOL

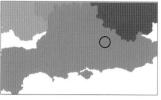

51° 17' 30" N, -0° 45' 12" E

16TH OCTOBER, 1908   TRENCHARD HOUSE, FARNBOROUGH ROAD, FARNBOROUGH, HAMPSHIRE, GU14 6TF

THE FIRST BRITISH AIRSHIP AND THE LANDMARK POWERED FLIGHT IN BRITAIN

Above: The Nulli Secundus II *airship, built using parts of the original* Nulli Secundus, *takes to the sky for its one and only flight on 14th August, 1908.*

Above: Nulli Secundus II is manoeuvred ready for take-off. The ship was fragile, however, and only made one 15-minute flight.

Like many technological inventions, the history of who did what first in the development of aviation is a complicated one. However, it is generally accepted that the first powered aircraft flight to take place in Britain happened at what was then the Balloon School at Farnborough in Hampshire, and the pilot was a colourful character called Samuel Franklin Cody.

Cody, an American who had moved to Britain, had worked as a cowboy and as a circus showman before touring Europe and then settling in Britain. After spending time as a showman, he became passionate about kites. He built a series of kites that were capable of lifting people; he then turned his attentions to gliders and later to airships.

During this time, Cody attracted the interest of the Admiralty, who were keen on the military possibilities of all these various flying machines and he became the chief instructor of kiting at the School of Ballooning. In 1907 Cody was part of the team that built the *Nulli Secundus* – the first British airship, which made a successful flight from Aldershot to London.

FLIMSY AIRCRAFT

Powered aircraft were Cody's next challenge and, after a series of earlier attempts in 1908, the first proper powered flight took place on 16th October. Cody had built his flimsy biplane – British Army Aeroplane No. 1 – largely of bamboo and canvas. It was similar to the American Wright brothers' plane, The Wright Flyer, with booms fore and aft to carry the elevator and rudder. It was powered by a 50hp Antoinette engine that drove two pusher propellers.

The historic flight lasted only 30 seconds. The plane flew at about 25 miles an hour for about 400 yards before it crashed. In the years that followed, Cody and the aviation world progressed to faster speeds, higher altitudes and longer flights. Sadly, Cody died in 1913 when his plane broke up in mid-air.

Cody's contribution is only one element of Farnborough's rich aviation history. Farnborough Airport remains a functioning airport and hosts the Farnborough airshow. The Cody Technology Park is home to a commercial company, formerly part of the Ministry of Defence, that conducts defence research.

A full-sized replica of British Army Aeroplane No. 1 is housed in the Farnborough Air Sciences Trust Museum. It was built to commemorate the centenary of the flight in 2008 and now stands in the Museum about 330 yards from the spot where the historic first step in British aviation took place.

Above: Samuel Cody in British Army Aeroplane No. 1 on 16th October, 1908, the day on which he made Britain's first powered flight.

Above: British Army Aeroplane No. 1 is pulled from the massive airship hangar at Farnborough prior to Cody's flight.

Above: Pulled by horses and the ground crew, the fragile machine, built from bamboo and canvas, is manoeuvred into take-off position.

Above: The newly completed Army airship Beta *is manoeuvred outside the Balloon Factory's hangar on Farnborough Common on 13th June, 1910.*

Above: Cody airborne in British Army Aeroplane No. 1 on 16th October, 1908. His flight lasted for 27 seconds and covered 1,390 feet.

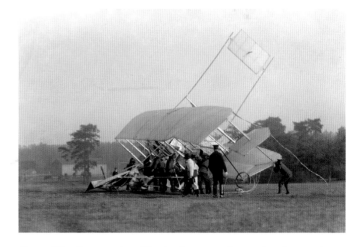

Above: Pilots have a saying: "Any landing you walk away from is a good one." Cody walked away from this and the machine was rebuilt.

HUNGERFORD
MASSACRE

51° 24' 41" N, 1° 30' 49" W

19TH AUGUST, 1987

SOUTH VIEW, HUNGERFORD, BERKSHIRE, RG17 0BX

MASS SHOOTING SPREE THAT CHANGED BRITISH GUN LAWS

Above: Smoke rises from Michael Ryan's home in Hungerford, which the gunman had set on fire after killing the family's pet dog. The blaze would destroy three neighbouring properties.

Just after 12.30pm on Wednesday, 19th August, 1987, Susan Godfrey was enjoying a picnic with her two young children in Savernake Forest in Wiltshire. Michael Ryan, an unemployed 27-year-old labourer from Hungerford, about seven miles away, approached Susan armed with a pistol and two semi-automatic rifles. He ordered her to put her children in the car, then took her into the bushes and shot her dead. The alarm was raised by a woman who discovered the children.

The murder of Susan Godfrey began a killing spree that lasted all afternoon. It left a total of 16 people

Above: Police marksmen prepare their equipment ready to tackle gunman Michael Ryan in Hungerford.

Above: Three days after Ryan's killing spree, quiet has returned to Hungerford's High Street, but the town would never be the same again.

dead and 15 others injured, and only ended with Ryan's suicide in the school where he'd been a pupil.

After killing Susan Godfrey, Ryan went back to Hungerford, shooting at a petrol-station cashier on the way, before returning to his home in South View. There he killed the family dog before setting the house ablaze. The resulting fire destroyed his home and three other properties.

RANDOM MURDERS

Ryan then set off on foot around his home town. His victims included two of his immediate neighbours, people walking their dogs, a police officer and, perhaps most gruesome of all, his own mother, who had returned to the scene to try to plead with her son. Some of Ryan's victims were shot in the street; others in their own homes. Late in the afternoon, Ryan broke into the John O'Gaunt Community Technology College, where he barricaded himself into a classroom. Police established contact with him and negotiations started, but just before 7pm that evening, he shot himself. Ryan's motives for the massacre have never been explained.

According to the official report by the chief constable, the police response to the events of that afternoon was hampered by several factors. The local 999 phone lines were overwhelmed by the number of calls.

Communications on the ground were unreliable.

Britain was stunned and shocked by the events of 19th August, 1987, which was the country's first modern peacetime experience of a mass shooting. There was a determination that such a thing should never be allowed to happen again. The Hungerford Massacre led to major changes in the law on the ownership of firearms. The official report into the incident revealed the shocking fact that Michael Ryan's arsenal of weapons was all held legally. Following Hungerford, semi-automatic weapons were banned and restrictions were placed on the use of shotguns. Sadly, these changes did not prevent subsequent shooting massacres at Dunblane in 1996 (see page 92) and in Cumbria in 2010.

Hungerford remembers the events of August 1987 quietly. There is a discreet memorial to those who died, but it is set away from the town centre near the football ground. During 2011 and 2012, the memorial was refurbished. The school where Ryan shot himself was repainted and reopened in time for the new term a few weeks after the shooting. The houses destroyed in the fire started by Ryan have been replaced.

In 2011 the Christmas lights in Hungerford were switched on by the Norwegian Ambassador. He had been invited by the Mayor of Hungerford, who recognised the common bond that existed between the town and Norway after the shootings on the island of Utøya in the summer of 2011 by Anders Breivik.

DISAPEARANCE IN
DEVON

50° 42' 43" N, 3° 22' 21" W

WITHIN LANE, AYLESBEARE, DEVON, EX5 2JQ

UNSOLVED MYSTERY OF A TEENAGER
WHO VANISHED

Above: A signpost pointing the way to Within Lane near Aylesbeare, where 13-year-old Genette Tate was abducted on 19th August, 1978.

W ithin Lane appears to be just another country lane in East Devon, not far from Exeter. However, it was the scene of a crime that has fascinated and haunted people for more than 30 years. It was there, on a quiet summer afternoon, that a teenage girl disappeared, leading to one of the largest and longest-running missing-person investigations in British history. To this day, no trace of the girl has been found, nor any useful clue to her disappearance.

Genette Tate, who was 13 years old, was delivering newspapers on Saturday, 19th August, 1978 around her home village of Aylesbeare. She was last seen alive by two friends at around 3.30pm. When they continued on their way a few moments later and turned a corner, they saw Genette's bike abandoned and newspapers strewn across the road.

SUSPECT QUESTIONED

A massive police search, assisted by an army of volunteers, was undertaken. Some local people reported seeing a maroon car in the area and police issued a photofit of a man they wanted to trace. Reconstructions of the moments leading to the disappearance took place. However, Genette's disappearance has never been explained and she has never been found.

Police have questioned convicted child killer Robert Black on a number of occasions about Genette Tate's vanishing and he has been considered a suspect in her case. However, he has denied any involvement in her abduction. In 2002, Genette's DNA was recovered from one of her sweaters retained by her mother since 1978, and police say that the investigation remains open.

On the 25th anniversary of Genette's disappearance, her parents, John Tate and Sheila Cook, who were divorced before their daughter vanished, both visited Within Lane. Both parents have said they believe that their daughter is dead.

There is a plaque and clock in the village hall given by police as a thank-you to the community for their help in the investigation. Genette's mother had a memorial stone erected in the village churchyard in Aylesbeare, which reads "In memory of Genette Louise Tate…May she someday be returned to this place to rest in peace."

Above: Sheila Cook, mother of Genette Tate, with her daughter's bicycle on which she had been delivering newspapers when she was snatched by an unknown assailant.

Left: Missing Devon schoolgirl Genette Tate, whose disappearance in August 1978 continues to baffle police.

SLAPTON SANDS
CALAMITY

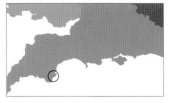

50° 16' 2" N, 3° 39' 8" W

SLAPTON SANDS BEACH, TORCROSS, DEVON, TQ7 2TQ

ALMOST A THOUSAND ALLIED SERVICEMEN KILLED IN A D-DAY REHEARSAL

Above: British troops training for the D-Day dash ashore from landing craft in the vicinity of Slapton Sands, Devon, on 6th May, 1944.

In an era where greater openness and transparency are generally the norm, it is difficult in the 21st century to understand how people kept the secrets of the Second World War for so many years. Those who worked as code breakers at Bletchley Park never spilt the beans until almost 30 years afterwards. Likewise, one of the most embarrassing incidents of the war, a D-Day rehearsal that went terribly wrong, remained largely secret until many years later.

Planning for the Allied invasion of France had begun long before its eventual execution in June 1944. The preparations and the rehearsals were extensive. One of the biggest rehearsals was Exercise Tiger, planned off the South Devon coast in late April 1944. Slapton Sands beach, near Dartmouth, was chosen because of its similarity to what became known as Utah Beach – one of the invasion points on the Normandy coast.

E-BOAT ATTACK

The Royal Navy was providing protection for the exercise with various ships stationed in Lyme Bay and also near to Cherbourg, where German motor torpedo boats, known as E-boats, were stationed. On the second day of the operation, Friday, 28th April, 1944, nine German E-boats spotted the exercise and attacked. A total of 638 American soldiers and sailors were killed and, in the chaos that followed, a further 308 died as a result of friendly fire. The British cruiser HMS *Hawkins* shelled the beach, apparently because the Supreme Allied Commander General Dwight D. Eisenhower had decided that it was necessary to create real battle conditions.

COVER UP

Ten officers who had special security clearance, and who knew the details of the planned D-Day landings, were lost in the incident. Until their bodies were found, the D-Day landings were nearly called off, because of a fear that the security of the operation could have been threatened if they had been captured alive. The incident revealed a series of failings in the planning for D-Day and valuable lessons were learnt.

The incident was covered up at the time and those who survived it were sworn to secrecy. The casualty figures were only released in August 1944, after the Normandy landings had taken place, and they were included as part of the overall D-Day casualty numbers.

For many years the incident was hardly spoken about, but it was the efforts of local resident Ken Small in the 1970s that led to the event being properly remembered and commemorated. He discovered a submerged tank left over from the incident and in 1984 raised it from the sea. The tank now stands as a memorial to the tragedy in the car park at Torness, and there is also a memorial near the beach at Slapton Sands.

Above: Slapton Sands beach, seen from the southern end. At top left is the lagoon that made the area similar to Utah Beach in Normandy.

Above: An American Sherman tank that was lost at sea during the Exercise Tiger debacle and raised in 1984 by local resident Ken Small.

TORREY CANYON
OIL SPILL

49° 53' 56" N, 6° 6' 20" W

18TH MARCH, 1967   SEVEN STONES REEF, BETWEEN CORNWALL AND THE ISLES OF SCILLY

THE FIRST MAJOR ECOLOGICAL DISASTER
CAPTURED ON TV

Above: Broken into several large sections, the Torrey Canyon
supertanker lies on the Seven Stones reef leaching her cargo of oil.

Above: Troops try to disperse the oil with detergent on a Cornish beach.

Above: Eventually the oil was set alight by bombing the wreck.

Subsequent ecological catastrophes may have pushed the *Torrey Canyon* from the memory, but it was one of the first such events to be captured on television, and it was a pivotal moment in raising the environmental consciousness of Britain.

On Saturday, 18th March, 1967 the Liberian-registered oil tanker *Torrey Canyon* was en route from the Canary Islands to Milford Haven in Wales. An inquiry concluded that the ship struck Pollard's Rock on Seven Stones Reef, between Cornwall and the Isles of Scilly, because the ship's master took a short cut to save time.

The consequences of this action were disastrous. The ship had a capacity of 120,000 tons, and oil from the vessel was washed up on 120 miles of the Cornish coast and 50 miles of the French coast. The oil slick measured 270 square miles and it is estimated that more than 15,000 birds were killed.

TANKER BOMBED

The attempts by the British authorities to contain the disaster were dramatic and not without problems. Detergents were sprayed on the slick and on beaches where oil had arrived, but it's thought that the detergents killed many birds rather than dispersing the oil. On 28th March, the Government decided on more radical action by setting fire to the oil. Forty-two 1,000lb bombs were dropped on the ship, which was breaking up on the rocks, to release the oil. Somewhat comically, many of the bombs missed their rather large target.

After the bombing, aviation fuel was dropped on the oil to set it alight, but it took several attempts to get the blaze going, eventually involving the use of napalm. Booms used in an attempt to contain the slick were largely ineffective because of high winds and rough seas. Eventually, the ship sank, but the havoc caused by the oil continued for a long time afterwards.

TRAGIC IMPACT

The oil slicks had a major impact on the fishing industry and on Cornish tourism, although it could have been much worse. The wind conditions at the time carried much of the slick away from Cornwall and sent it towards the Brittany coast and on to the Channel Islands.

The *Torrey Canyon* disaster led to new international regulations that placed tougher responsibilities on shipping companies. Eventually, compensation was paid to both the British and French Governments by the ship's owners.

The wreck of the *Torrey Canyon* lies 100 feet below the sea near Seven Stones reef and is visited by deep sea divers. There's another lasting legacy of the disaster in Guernsey. When the slick arrived there, much of the oil was dumped in a quarry in the north of the island, now known locally as Torrey Canyon Quarry. Although much of the oil has been removed, more than 40 years later the authorities in Guernsey are still trying to dispose of the remnants of the oil safely and in an environmentally acceptable way.

MARCONI'S
WIRELESS STATION

12TH DECEMBER, 1901   THE MARCONI CENTRE, POLDHU, NEAR MULLION, CORNWALL, TR12 7JB.

FIRST TRANSATLANTIC RADIO MESSAGE

Above: During the First World War, Guglielmo Marconi was given the rank of lieutenant and put in charge of the Italian Army's radio service.

A s you walk the coastal path on the Lizard Peninsula in Cornwall, you come across the remains of a site whose significance in the history of communications is difficult to overstate. It was here in December 1901 at Poldhu, between Mullion and Porthleven, that Guglielmo Marconi's project to transmit the first transatlantic radio signal succeeded.

Marconi, who was born in Bologna in Italy in 1874, had come to England at the age of 21 because he thought it would be easier to attract support and funds for his radio experiments than in Italy.

Left: A plaque commemorating Marconi's achievement at the Poldhu site. It was presented by the company that bears his name in 1955.

Above: The Marconi Centre, home to a museum and radio club.

The 50-acre site at Poldhu was bought by Marconi in 1900 and work began to build the transmitting station for the transatlantic experiment. Marconi chose the site because of its remoteness so that he could keep his preparations out of the public eye. The original ring of masts was destroyed in a storm in September 1901 and a temporary fan-shaped aerial supported by two masts was erected within a week.

FAINT SIGNAL

It was arranged that the Poldhu station would transmit the letter 'S' in Morse code from 3pm to 6pm each day from 10th December, 1901. It was at 4pm (12.30pm Newfoundland local time) on Thursday, 12th December that the faint signal transmitted from Poldhu was received by Marconi on the other side of the Atlantic at a temporary station established at Signal Hill, St John's – a distance of over 2,200 miles. The signal confounded the sceptics who had doubted that wireless signals could be sent across such great distances.

Marconi's achievement was the culmination of almost half a century of experimentation by many scientists. He is credited with having the determination and the resources to pursue the dream of wireless telegraphy, although he didn't invent anything new.

There were some who doubted that Marconi's claim to have transmitted a signal over such a distance was genuine, as there was no independent verification of it. However, the Poldhu experiment in 1901 is now generally accepted as marking the moment when the

Above: The monument at Poldhu commemorating Marconi's historic transmission of a radio signal across the Atlantic.

long-distance transmission of messages without wires became a reality. In that sense, it was the forerunner of the many developments in communications that followed throughout the remainder of the 20th century, including radio broadcasting, satellites, mobile phones and the internet.

Marconi continued to use the Poldhu station for a variety of other radio experiments until it closed in 1933. The site was dismantled, but parts of the concrete base of the transmitting station remain and there is a monument commemorating the 1901 event. In 2001 a small museum, the Marconi Centre, was opened near the site – a joint effort by the Poldhu Amateur Radio Club, the Marconi Company and the National Trust who now own the site.

FILTON
AERODROME

THE BIRTHPLACE OF CONCORDE

Above: The British Concorde prototype (002) lifts off on its first flight from the runway at Filton, near Bristol, on 9th April, 1969.

Concorde conjures up all sorts of images – glamorous supersonic travel, celebrities, cutting-edge technology, Anglo-French co-operation and much more. Yet this product of the age of technological optimism in the 1960s, which was heralded as the future of air travel, was to be a short-lived phenomenon. It burst on to the scene in the late 1960s, literally soared into the sky, but just over 30 years later the dream, and the planes, were grounded to become museum pieces.

The Concorde project had its origins in the 1950s, when a number of countries began research into the idea of supersonic air travel. In 1962, the British and French governments decided to collaborate on the project, principally to reduce costs. The treaty led to a partnership between the British Aircraft Corporation

(BAC) and the French company Aerospatiale, and work began on both sides of the English Channel in 1965 on two prototypes.

BRITISH BASE

Filton Aerodrome, or Bristol Filton Airport as it later became, was at the centre of the British end of the partnership. Parts for Concorde were made at a variety of locations, but Filton was the centre and it was from there that the completed prototype first took to the skies.

The French prototype (001) made its first test flight in March 1969, to be followed by the British prototype (002). On Wednesday, 9th April, 1969, a former RAF pilot, Brian Trubshaw, flew 002 from Filton to RAF Fairford, Gloucester. Both planes were then presented publicly at the Paris Air Show in June 1969. The first supersonic flights took place later that year.

Despite the excitement of those pioneering days, Concorde was beset by problems almost from the outset. Many of the countries that had originally expressed an interest in buying the plane changed their minds. There were concerns about the noise, the environmental impact and the commercial viability.

Although a few other airlines did dabble with Concorde, in the end only British Airways and Air France maintained a regular service. Both airlines ran scheduled flights between Europe and the United States. Concorde could cross the Atlantic in 3 hours 20 minutes, less than half the time of a conventional subsonic aircraft.

The aircraft's final demise started in 2000, when an Air France Concorde crashed near Paris, killing all 100 passengers and nine crew on board, as well as four people on the ground. All Concordes were grounded pending the outcome of an investigation, which subsequently concluded that the cause of the crash was a tyre being punctured by a titanium alloy strip. The strip had broken off a plane that had taken off earlier from the same runway at Charles de Gaulle Airport.

Concorde did resume flying the following year, but in 2003 Air France and British Airways announced that they were taking the airliner out of service. Concorde undertook a series of farewell flights around Britain in October 2003.

CONCORDE GROUNDED

In total, 20 Concordes were built. Six were prototypes and 14 entered service. Of these 14, one crashed and one was cannibalised for spare parts. The other 12 still exist and six are now on display at various museums.

As with Concorde itself, its home of Filton is also facing retirement. Its history as an aviation centre goes back more than a century. Opened in 1910, it became a base for the Royal Flying Corps in the First World War. In the Second World War, it played an important role as a base for American forces prior to, and after, D-Day. After the war it was extended to allow work on the Brabazon, an earlier ultimately unsuccessful aircraft project, and then further extended for Concorde in the 1960s.

Part of the airfield was redeveloped as housing in 2006. In 2011 BAE Systems, which owns Filton, announced that it would close the airfield at the end of 2012. There are plans for a business park and further housing with some heritage elements, including one surviving Concorde, retained on the site. However, a local protest group was formed to try to save the airfield from closure.

Left: Beaming test pilot Brian Trubshaw after completing the first flight in Concorde. "It was wizard, a cool, calm and collected operation," he said.

Far left: A mock-up of Concorde is shown at Filton on 24th February, 1967.

THE GREAT TRAIN
ROBBERY

51° 48' 6" N, 1° 3' 23" W

LEATHERSLADE FARM, NEAR OAKLEY, BUCKINGHAMSHIRE, HP18 9SG

THE FARM WHERE THE ROBBERS
COUNTED THE CASH

Above: The mail train abandoned by the gang at the bridge where they audaciously unloaded £2.6m into a waiting truck on 8th August, 1963.

Up a farm track, near the village of Oakley, in the Buckinghamshire countryside, stands a modern house set among a group of trees that looks entirely unremarkable. However, it was on this site half a century ago that the perpetrators of probably the most famous crime in 20th-century Britain laid low immediately after committing their heist.

The Great Train Robbery has acquired an aura and romance that still sets it apart from other crimes. Indeed, its perpetrators have often been portrayed as loveable rogues in a way that rather ignores the fact that they used considerable violence in carrying out their crime. However, the scale and audacity of the robbery at the time, and the subsequent escapes and flights from justice of some of the robbers, have made this crime something that continues to fascinate 50 years on.

In the early morning of Thursday, 8th August,

1963, the gang attacked the Glasgow-to-London mail train, which had set off the previous evening with 12 carriages and over 70 Post Office staff, who sorted mail during the journey. One of the carriages was designated the HVP (High Value Packages) Coach, where mail containing money was transported. The value of the money on board, £2.6m (equivalent to around £40m in 2012), was apparently unusually high because it followed a bank holiday weekend in Scotland.

Just after 3am, the train stopped at a red light near Sears Crossing near Ledburn, between Leighton Buzzard and Cheddington. The robbers had tampered with the signals and, when the co-driver got out of the train to telephone the signal box, he was pushed down the embankment by the waiting gang members. The train then had to be moved along the track to a bridge where the gang's truck was waiting. The train driver, Jack Mills,

Above: The engine and coaches of the train are held under police guard at Cheddington Station in Buckinghamshire on the day after the robbery.

was ordered to move the train, but was hit over the head after initially being reluctant to do so. The gang's original plan to use a replacement driver was foiled when he proved unable to operate the particular type of locomotive.

Once the train was moved to Bridego Bridge, the gang, consisting of 15 members, overwhelmed the postal workers inside the HVP coach and unloaded more than 120 sacks into their waiting truck. About half an hour after the robbery began, they fled the scene and drove about 20 miles to their hideaway, Leatherslade Farm. The farm was run down and had been bought two months earlier for use in the robbery.

The gang's original plan had been to stay at Leatherslade Farm until Sunday, but they left on the Friday, after just one day there, because it became obvious to them that the police knew that they had stayed in the area. While at the farm, as well as dividing up the cash, they apparently played Monopoly to pass the time – but using real money.

The police discovered the farm four days later, on Tuesday, 13th August. The getaway vehicles, mailbags, money wrappers, as well as food and sleeping bags and the Monopoly set, were found. Although the gang had tried to rid the farm of evidence, police did discover some fingerprints.

Above: Leatherslade Farm, where the gang laid low for a day after the robbery. They left two Land Rovers and a truck there, as well as vital evidence.

Most of the gang members were caught over a period of months up to the end of 1963 and their trial began in Aylesbury on 20th January, 1964. The trial ended in April 1964 with nearly all the gang convicted and most sentenced to terms of 20 or 30 years imprisonment. Some had their sentences reduced on appeal.

Several of the members of the gang acquired even greater notoriety by fleeing from justice or by escaping from prison after they were sentenced. Bruce Reynolds went to Mexico and then returned to Britain to be arrested in Torquay. After serving his sentence, 'Buster' Edwards famously set up a flower stall outside Waterloo Station, but died in 1994 apparently having committed suicide. Charlie Wilson was shot dead, apparently related to drugs, in his villa in Marbella. Ronnie Biggs is probably the best known. He returned to Britain voluntarily after his long exile abroad in France, then Australia and mainly in Brazil, and was returned to prison, but he was released on compassionate grounds in 2009.

The train driver, Jack Mills, suffered health problems after the robbery and died in 1970. The second driver, David Whitby, died from a heart attack in 1972.

The hideaway is no more. In 1995, a new owner of Leatherslade Farm demolished the buildings where the robbers had hidden and built a new house on the site.

Left: Some of the gang, L–R: Bruce Reynolds, who planned the robbery; Douglas Goody, considered second in command; Ronald 'Buster' Edwards, a professional criminal and key organiser of the raid; Ronnie Biggs, probably the most well known of the train robbers, but who actually played only a minor role..

Above: The dilapidated farmhouse at Leatherslade Farm. It was there that the gang played Monopoly with real money – and left their fingerprints.

GREENHAM
COMMON

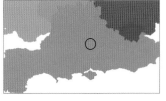

1981–2000   GREENHAM COMMON, NEWBURY, BERKSHIRE, RG19 6HW

THE SCENE OF ONE OF BRITAIN'S LONGEST-RUNNING PROTESTS

Above: Protestors form a continuous human chain around the American cruise missile base at Greenham Common on 12th December, 1982.

Greenham Common air base witnessed one of the longest-running and most sustained protests in British history. Protestors, mainly but not exclusively women, maintained a camp outside the base against the deployment of nuclear missiles there from 1981 and continued it until 2000, long after the missiles had left.

The origin of the protest was the decision by the British government in 1980 to allow American cruise missiles to be stationed at a number of sites, including RAF Greenham Common, during the Cold War. The first protest at Greenham Common occurred in late 1981. From then on there was a series of blockades of the camp, the first in May 1982.

HUMAN CHAIN

The protest at Greenham came to public attention on 1st April, 1983, when a 14-mile human chain of 70,000 protestors was formed from Greenham to the military installations at Aldermaston and Burghfield. Following this, peace camps were established at other sites in Britain and elsewhere.

The development of the airfield to accommodate the missiles went ahead and six massive shelters designed to withstand direct hits were built. From then on there was a cat-and-mouse game between protestors and the authorities. There were numerous attempts to end the blockade and to break up the protest. The local council, Newbury District Council, attempted to evict the protestors on more than one occasion, but their efforts were in vain. The protest simply reformed. At its height, there were nine major camps stationed near the different gates of the base and scores of other camps.

PERIMETER BREACHED

Over the years, there were many arrests. Protestors chained themselves to the perimeter fence and the boundary was breached many times. The protests divided public and media opinion.

The cruise missiles were removed from Greenham in 1991 as a result of the Intermediate Range Forces Treaty, but the camp remained. The protest turned into more general opposition to Britain's own nuclear weapons programme, in particular the Trident system. In 1992, the air base was declared redundant, and in 1997 it was bought by the Greenham Common Trust. Much of the site of the airfield has been returned to common land. A business park was established on part of the site, which contains 150 businesses. The silos where the cruise missiles were stored remain on the site, but are fenced off from the common land and the business park.

The history of the site is acknowledged. There is a memorial to the protest near the main entrance to the new park. The trust is funding a memorial to commemorate the lives of American servicemen killed in accidents there during the war.

Above: Greenham Common in 1999, by which time much of it had been turned into a business park and common land open to the public.

Above: Protestors in their camp outside the base's 'Yellow Gate' on 26th August, 1983. There were several similar camps around the perimeter.

FORT BELVEDERE

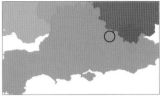

51° 24' 15" N, -0° 36' 43" E

WHERE THE ABDICATION CRISIS WAS PLAYED OUT IN 1936

Above: Fort Belvedere in August 1929, just before Edward, Prince of Wales moved in. He commissioned a considerable amount of interior renovation.

Seventy years later the notion that there should have been such a furore over the idea that the King might marry a divorcée seems a little surreal. But in 1936, King Edward VIII's desire to marry the twice-married American Wallis Simpson threatened the future of the British monarchy and caused a constitutional crisis.

What's more, in a much more deferential era of media ethics, it was only at the very height of the crisis, and very close to the abdication itself, in December 1936, that the British public were even made aware that the new King was in a relationship with a married woman.

The abdication is probably located in many people's minds at Windsor Castle. It was from there that, on Friday, 11th December, the King made his famous abdication radio address, including the celebrated line

"I have found it impossible to carry the heavy burden of responsibility and to discharge my duties as King as I would wish to do without the help and support of the woman I love."

However, most of the events leading up to the abdication were played out a few miles away from Windsor Castle, on the other side of Windsor Great Park, at Fort Belvedere. The fort had been built between 1750 and 1755 for Prince William Augustus, the Duke of Cumberland, who was the younger son of George II. It enjoyed a view over Virginia Water and was used as a summer house. Various alterations were made over the years to the house by a succession of members of the Royal family. In 1911 it was converted into a residence.

In 1930, King George V gave Fort Belvedere to his

Above: King Edward VIII makes the historic radio broadcast from Windsor Castle, telling the nation of his plan to abdicate on 11th December, 1936.

Above: Shocked Londoners read of the King's decision to give up the throne to marry Mrs Wallis Simpson on the day that the abdication was announced.

son Edward, the Prince of Wales. It remained his main residence from then until the abdication. It was here that he entertained Wallis Simpson, whom he'd met in 1934. When his father died in January 1936, Edward became King. He had already decided that he wanted to marry Mrs Simpson.

IMPOSSIBLE MARRIAGE

Throughout 1936, the crisis gradually developed – largely unknown by most of the British public – with the British establishment largely of the view that it was impossible for the King to marry a woman who was already divorced from her first husband and wanting a

divorce from her second. This view was strengthened because the King was head of the Church of England, which, at the time, did not permit remarriage of divorcees. The fact that Simpson was an American was also a concern to some people.

It was almost certainly also the case that many politicians were keen to see Edward forced to resign because they thought him unsuitable to be King. In 1936, the threat of Nazi Germany was already apparent and Edward, with his record of womanising and his apparent lack of seriousness, was seen by some as a liability.

It was at Fort Belvedere that most of the key events that led to the abdication took place. These included meetings between the King and his advisors and, most

Above: The Duke and Duchess of Windsor at Charters in Sunninghill, Berkshire, where they were staying with friends Mr and Mrs Parkinson, in May 1947.

crucially, between the King and Prime Minister Stanley Baldwin. Eventually, on Thursday, 10th December, Edward signed the abdication order, the first British monarch to do so. His brother succeeded him as King George VI.

NAZI SYMPATHIES

The day after the abdication broadcast, Edward left Fort Belvedere for the last time and travelled to France, where he married Wallis Simpson the following year. For the rest of their lives Edward, who was made Duke of Windsor, and his wife lived away from Britain, mainly in France, although he served as Governor of Bermuda during the Second World War. In 1937, the couple had met Adolf Hitler and they were widely considered to have Nazi sympathies. Hitler was said to have planned to install them as monarchs if Germany had successfully invaded Britain.

Later in life, there was a partial reconciliation with the Royal family and the couple did return to Britain on a number of occasions, but not, as far as is known, to Fort Belvedere. The duke died in 1972 and the duchess in 1986. Both are buried in Windsor Great Park in the Royal burial ground.

Fort Belvedere was used as government offices during the Second World War. It remains the property of the Crown Estate, but has been rented as a private home by a succession of tenants since the 1950s.

GRUNWICK STRIKERS
PICKETING

51° 32' 50" N, -0° 14' 49" E

20TH AUGUST, 1976   CHAPTER ROAD AND COBBOLD ROAD, WILLESDEN, LONDON, NW10 9SU

A DEFINING INDUSTRIAL DISPUTE
OF THE 1970s

Above: Police struggle to hold back hundreds of pickets as a bus carrying non-striking workers approaches the Grunwick plant.

Bitter and sometimes violent industrial disputes characterised the 1970s and 1980s in Britain. What happened at a photographic processing firm in the backstreets of North London in the mid-1970s was one of the most significant industrial disputes of the era, which shaped trade union law and attitudes for years to come. For people on both the left and the right, it was a defining moment.

In many ways, what made Grunwick stand out was the fact that most of the people involved in the strike were Asian women. Until then the popular image of

strikers was of a highly unionised, largely white, male workforce exercising its industrial muscle. The Grunwick workforce was around 90 per cent black and Asian, and most were female.

Grunwick's business was the processing of photographs via the post. Previously, high-street chemists had monopolised the photo processing market, but the growth of photography as a pastime offered new business possibilities, and the Grunwick Film Processing Laboratories, set up in 1965 by George Ward, was one of the companies exploiting this opportunity. Grunwick had two premises in Willesden – at Chapter Road and Cobbold Road. Most accounts agree that the premises were in decent condition, but the official report held into the dispute later concluded that, prior to the strike, wages were below average.

UNION RECOGNITION

The dispute began on Friday, 20th August of that year when colleagues walked out in support of one of the workers who had been dismissed for working too slowly at the Chapter Road plant. The strike leader, Jayaben Desai, became the iconic symbol of the dispute, and she and her workmates were labelled 'strikers in saris' by the media.

What followed was a long and bitter dispute that lasted two years. The strikers started a picket of the premises demanding union recognition. The wider union movement and the political left swung in behind the strikers. Arthur Scargill, president of the Yorkshire area of the National Union of Mineworkers, and representatives of the miners' union, joined the picket. The local Conservative MP and the right-wing National Association for Freedom backed Grunwick. There were violent clashes between police and pickets outside the factories. More than a hundred workers at Grunwick were dismissed during the dispute.

Legal action ensued, the conciliation service ACAS got involved and, eventually, an official inquiry by Lord Scarman recommended union recognition and reinstatement of the strikers. Jayaben Desai and colleagues went on hunger strike during the dispute to try to get the Trades Union Congress to back the strikers unambiguously. However, in the face of weakening support from unions who were worried about legal action, the dispute ended on 14th July, 1978, when the strikers called off their picket. They were not reinstated and union recognition had not been achieved.

STRUGGLE OR DEFEAT?

On the right, the Grunwick dispute is often portrayed as a victory over unbridled union power and seen as paving the way for the trade union reforms instituted by Margaret Thatcher's government in the 1980s. For the left, the dispute is remembered as an epic struggle by marginalised workers standing up for their rights.

Grunwick moved away from Willesden after the dispute to Hertfordshire. The strike leader, Jayaben Desai, died in 2010 and the company chairman, George Ward, died in 2012. The Chapter Road site, which was owned by Brent Council, was later used by a variety of voluntary organisations, but it was replaced by flats. The Cobbold Road site is now part of a small industrial estate.

Above: Violence breaks out again during the Grunwick dispute as police officers manhandle pickets who had come from all over the country.

Above: Police guard the plant entrance. This was the first time that the paramilitary Special Patrol Group had been used in an industrial dispute.

JOHN LOGIE BAIRD'S
SOHO LOFT

51° 30' 48" N, -0° 7' 52" E

26TH JANUARY, 1926   BAR ITALIA, 22 FRITH STREET, LONDON, W1D 4RT

THE FIRST PUBLIC DEMONSTRATION OF TV

Above: John Logie Baird demonstrates his electro-mechanical 'Televisor' to members of the Royal Institution and the press on 26th January, 1926.

In the hustle and bustle of Soho in central London, halfway along Frith Street, there's yet another coffee shop. But behind the façade of the Bar Italia is the legacy of a key event in the development of television. What was to culminate in the start of a public 'high-definition' television service in Britain a decade later from Alexandra Palace in November 1936 (see page 52) had its origins here in the mid-1920s.

We feel a need to pinpoint dates and to simplify the stories of the invention of new developments, whereas the truth is nearly always far more complicated. A number of people from several different countries contributed to the development of what became known as television over a period of many years, stretching back into the latter part of the 19th century. However, there's no doubt that John Logie Baird was the first person to show a recognisable television picture and deserves the recognition for his central role in the arrival of TV.

PICTURE TRANSMISSION

From 1923, first in Hastings, East Sussex, and then at Frith Street in Soho, Baird worked on developing television, building on the work of earlier pioneers who had successfully transmitted still pictures over distances. In March and April 1925 he held a public demonstration inside Selfridge's department store in London, showing the transmission of silhouette images. On 2nd October, 1925, he transmitted what is regarded as the first real

television picture – the head of a ventriloquist's dummy named 'Stooky Bill' on a 32-line-resolution picture and then repeated the experiment with a real person – an office worker called William Taynton. However, like many inventors and pioneers, Baird had to contend with scepticism. He tried to get publicity for his ideas, but was often rebuffed. The news editor of the *Daily Express* is reportedly said to have dismissed him as a "lunatic".

Baird persisted, and on Tuesday, 26th January, 1926, he organised a demonstration in front of 40 members of the Royal Institution and a reporter from *The Times,* where he transmitted pictures of his guests from one room to another in his Soho workshop. This was a key moment in Baird's campaign to get people interested in what many considered a scientific fantasy. It took almost another decade before the Government took television seriously and set up a committee to look into it.

BIRTH OF TELEVISION

In 1929, the first regular public television broadcasts were carried out using the Baird 30-line electro-mechanical system and existing BBC voice transmitters. Programmes were made initially by the Baird Company, but in 1932 the BBC formally agreed to take over programme making. The audience was largely comprised of radio enthusiasts who had built their own 'Televisors' from kits and parts. In 1935, the low-definition service was shut down and, in hindsight, written off as 'experimental' when television moved into its next phase in 1936.

Sadly, for the man regarded as the main television pioneer, Baird's partly mechanical TV system was superseded by the Marconi-EMI fully electrical system, once the public service got under way in 1936. Nevertheless, had it not been for the work of Baird in his Soho loft, television's arrival would have been delayed and may not have been the powerful medium it is today.

Above: The building in Frith Street, Soho, where John Logie Baird continued his work on television that had begun in Hastings.

WHITE CITY
STADIUM

51° 30' 43" N, -0° 13' 29" E

24TH JULY, 1908

WOOD LANE, LONDON, W12 7TQ

A SPECTACULAR EXHIBITION AND THE
SITE OF BRITAIN'S FIRST OLYMPIC GAMES

Today, Wood Lane in West London is home to two very well-known, but rather different, global brands – the BBC and the Westfield Shopping Centre. A century ago what was then an area of industrial scrubland was turned into an enormous exhibition ground complete with a major stadium that was to host the 1908 Olympic Games – the first Olympics held in Britain.

When work on the site first started, there was no talk of the Olympics being held there. The grounds were built to host the Franco-British Exhibition, conceived as a way of celebrating the Entente Cordiale, a friendship and collaboration agreement signed between Britain and France in 1904. It was intended to be a showcase of the glories of both countries and their empires. The 140-acre site was acquired in what was then an outlying area of West London with the intention of staging the exhibition in 1907.

Events elsewhere intervened. Rome had been due to stage the 1908 Olympics, but the eruption of Mount Vesuvius in April 1906 meant that the Italian Government decided it needed to divert funds to rebuild Naples – so the games were looking for a new venue. London offered and was chosen, and a deal was struck between the exhibition organisers and the Olympics to accommodate both events at the same site. As a result, the exhibition was delayed a year and both were staged in 1908.

TWIN ATTRACTIONS

The exhibition ran from May until October and was open from 10am until 11.15pm every day except Sundays. It attracted a staggering eight million visitors. The main features of the exhibition grounds were the array of ornate buildings painted white, giving rise to the name White City. The buildings contained exhibits and artefacts of all sorts from Britain and France and from countries across the

Thousands of spectators pack the stands of the newly-built, vast White City Stadium during the 1908 Olympic Games.

Above: A Mughal-style palace built around a lake was but one of the attractions created for the Franco-British Exhibition at White City in 1908.

British and French empires. There were gardens, an artificial lake, a scenic railway and a 'Flip-Flap' – two cars suspended high in the air on cantilevered arms affording a view over London.

The majority of the Olympic events were held in a two-week period in July. The Great Stadium, at the northern end of the exhibition park, was the main focus of the games. The stadium, which could accommodate 68,000 people seated and more than 100,000 in total, was built in less than ten months at a cost of £60,000 (around £6m at 2012 prices). The swimming and diving pools were located in the middle of the stadium inside the running track.

Twenty-two nations took part in the games in 24 different sporting disciplines. Great Britain won most medals. The games were the first since the revival of the modern Olympiad in 1896 to be filmed and they were not without controversy. There were complaints about the quality of the British hospitality, particularly from the Americans. There were allegations that the sports officials, who were all British, were biased. Some countries refused to dip their flags to the British King, Edward VII, during the opening ceremony.

DISPUTED MARATHON

The most famous incident of the games occurred on 24th July, at the end of the marathon when Italian runner Dorando Pietri, who was the first to enter the stadium at the end of the course from Windsor Great Park, collapsed yards from the finish line. He was helped to his feet by officials and managed to stagger across the finishing line ahead of American Johnny Hayes. However, Pietri was later disqualified because he had been assisted.

PREMIER DOG TRACK

After the exhibition and the games of 1908, the White City Stadium lived on. In 1927, it started hosting greyhound racing and remained one of the premier tracks in the country until 1984. In 1932 the athletics track was refurbished and for the next 40 years White City was the home of the Amateur Athletics Championships until they moved to Crystal Palace.

The stadium hosted a range of other sports, including football. One game in the 1966 World Cup, between Uruguay and France, was held at White City because Wembley, where it should have been played, refused to cancel a regular Friday-night greyhound racing meeting.

A number of films were shot at the stadium and concerts were held there. The exhibition grounds had proved so popular that seven further exhibitions were held there before the outbreak of the First World War in 1914. The exhibition buildings were progressively demolished and, in the 1930s, a large part of the site was cleared for housing.

TV TAKES OVER

After the Second World War, the BBC acquired part of the site to build a new centre for its television operation. BBC Television Centre opened in June 1960. This building has been the main home to most of the BBC's TV (and some radio) output ever since, but in 2011 the BBC confirmed that the building was up for sale. In 2008, the giant Westfield Shopping Centre opened on the other side of Wood Lane on land that had also been part of the original Franco-British Exhibition site.

The White City Stadium closed in 1984, being demolished and replaced by further BBC buildings. The 1908 Olympics are commemorated outside the entrance with a mural that is said to be on the finish line of the marathon. One of the streets in the area is named Dorando Close after the disqualified marathon runner, and South Africa Road is on the site of the exhibition's South African Pavilion.

Although there are few visible signs left of the sporting and entertainment heritage of this site, White City is a strong example of how public spaces fashioned for great events find new uses – in this case from sport and exhibitions to shopping and television.

Above: Controversy is sparked as Italian marathon runner Dorando Pietri is helped over the line by well-meaning officials. He was disqualified.

Above: An artist's impression of the stadium with the Franco-British Exhibition site beyond. Such a vast project seems unimaginable today.

Above: The exhibition's popular 'Flip-Flap' ride, which gave the intrepid a view of the whole site from an aerial vantage point.

THE MILLENNIUM
DOME

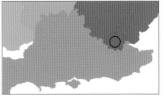

51° 30' 6" N, 0° 0' 11" E

31ST DECEMBER, 1999

THE O2 ARENA, MILLENNIUM WAY, GREENWICH, LONDON, SE10 0BB

BRITAIN'S MILLENNIUM CELEBRATION AT A COST OF £750 MILLION

Above: With the site on the Greenwich Peninsula marked out, work begins in October 1997 on erecting the 12 pylons that would support the dome.

Above: By December 1998, the basic dome structure was complete and stood in stark contrast to the office blocks that formed the City skyline.

The Crystal Palace was the first place featured on this journey and it's fitting that the Millennium Dome should be the last. They share certain characteristics. Both were originally built for great celebratory events – the 1851 Great Exhibition and the 2000 Millennium respectively. Both had question marks about their future once the event for which they had been built was over.

An abiding image of the Millennium Dome is the picture of the Queen and then Prime Minister Tony Blair rather awkwardly holding hands and singing *Auld Lang Syne* to usher in the new Millennium at midnight on Friday, 31st December, 1999. The political machinations that produced the tent-like structure on reclaimed land on the banks of the Thames at Greenwich, in which this moment of national celebration took place, had begun several years before.

TOXIC CLEAR UP

The land on which the dome came to be built was previously occupied by the East Greenwich Gasworks, which shut in 1985, leaving a legacy of toxic sludge. The reclamation of the area had begun in the late 1980s,

but it was under John Major's Conservative Government that the idea of a Festival of Britain-style celebration of the new Millennium was first agreed. In 1996, the Greenwich site was chosen ahead of rival bids from several places, including the NEC in Birmingham and Pride Park in Derby.

One of the first decisions the incoming Labour Government under Tony Blair had to make when it was elected in 1997 was whether to embrace the project or

Above: An awkward moment? The Queen holds hands with the Duke of Edinburgh and Tony Blair during a rendition of Auld Lang Syne.

Above: With 400 days to go before the official opening of the dome on New Year's Eve, 1999, the organisers celebrate by lighting up the structure.

abandon it. There were strong voices within the Cabinet arguing for the latter. However, Blair was personally committed to the idea of an upbeat celebration of the Millennium and the decision was taken to go ahead.

The project was dogged by escalating costs and political controversy. Its eventual cost was over £750m and it was widely criticised as being too expensive and a waste of what was largely public money. Despite the controversy, the construction continued and the structure was completed in June 1999.

ZONES OF LIFE

The dome was designed by Richard Rogers. Its tent-like structure is full of horological symmetry. It has 12 100m high support towers, one for each month of the year. The canopy is 52 metres high in the middle, one metre for every week of the year and it is 365 metres in diameter, one metre for every day of the year. The idea of the dome was to create a vast space, inside which a celebration of national life could take place. The Millennium Experience was split into 14 zones under the three broad themes of Who We Are, What We Do and Where We Live. These exhibition areas were located around a central performance area, where a daily Millennium Show was performed. There were other associated shows and attractions around the dome, including a play area called Timekeepers of the Millennium. There was criticism that some of the zones lacked content, but the visitor response was generally favourable and the dome was the most popular tourist attraction in Britain that year.

On its opening night, the dome received bad press. This was probably because many VIPs, including media executives, were kept waiting for hours because of ticketing problems. However, the public reception proved to be less hostile.

Above: Early on New Year's Eve, 1999, final rehearsals take place in the dome for the stage show that will welcome the new Millennium.

Despite welcoming 6.5 million visitors during its year of opening, the total was a long way short of the 12 million visitors on which the attraction's financial planning had been based.

After the Millennium Experience closed on 31st December, 2000, the exhibits were removed. Some were taken back by the original producers. Chessington World of Adventures acquired the Timekeepers of the Millennium attraction, and various souvenirs and memorabilia ended up at Dreamland in Margate.

DOME REBORN

Thereafter, there was continuing controversy about what should happen to the building. Before it had opened there was an idea that it could become a football stadium, but that came to nothing. For three years it was empty, apparently costing £1m a month to maintain. A number of temporary events took place, including the Winter Wonderland show in 2003 and one-off music events organised by the Mayor of London.

Ideas for its future use included its redevelopment as a business park or its conversion into a sports complex with housing around it. But in 2005 work began on turning the dome into a major entertainment centre. A naming rights deal led to it becoming the O2 Arena on 31st May that year. In June 2007 it reopened as a multi-purpose entertainment centre, including a concert hall, an exhibition space, a cinema, an arena and a host of bars and restaurants. During the 2012 London Olympic Games, O2's naming rights were suspended and the dome became the North Greenwich Arena, being used for gymnastics, trampoline and basketball.

More than a decade on from the Millennium, the controversy that surrounded the dome had faded and one of the most recognisable landmarks in Britain had reinvented itself.

CONCLUSION

"...one crowded hour of glorious life is worth an age without a name."

Sir Walter Scott

Above: Sir Roger Bannister rings the bell on the last lap of the Men's One Mile Elite Race at the Iffley Road sports ground on 6th May, 2004 to celebrate the 50th anniversary of his sub-four minute mile.

Places are like people. They reinvent themselves when circumstances change. They react in a variety of ways when tragedy strikes. Sometimes, but not always, they come to terms with what happens. Some make a song and dance about their achievements and their disasters. Others guard their stories modestly or silently. Although the places featured on this journey and the events they bore witness to are disparate, there are some conclusions to be drawn.

For those places where tragic events have taken place, the process of coming to terms with what happened can, of course, never properly end. What happened in Aberfan, Dunblane, Lockerbie and Hungerford won't be forgotten, even after people directly involved and affected have moved elsewhere or died. However, time does make a difference. The more distant an event, the more it can be viewed as history and less as current affairs.

So Aberfan, for example, almost 50 years ago, is fully part of Welsh history and taught in schools, and the memorial gardens there have a steady stream of visitors

who, it would appear, are an accepted fact of life in the community. Even in places where more recent disasters occurred, such as Dunblane and Lockerbie, people visit out of curiosity and respect and, by and large, do so without causing resentment.

It is also clearly the case that strong community bonds have been formed out of such tragedies and that they have been sustained for many years after the events. Inevitably, in the aftermath of such events, there have been divisions within communities, for example between the families of victims and those unaffected. However, it would appear that in all the places touched by tragedy, the sense of community has increased. In Lockerbie and Dunblane, new community facilities have been built in response to the disasters and have become a focus for a stronger sense of place.

In some cases, though, the priority is demolition not construction. Sometimes there is an urge to get rid of the specific location of distressing events partly to avoid prurient interest, but also because the events were so awful that it is impossible to imagine the spot where they occurred being put comfortably to any other future

Above: A historic site was reborn in Arsenal's former home, Highbury Stadium. The basic structure of the elegant art deco stands was retained and redeveloped into a complex of luxury accommodation, with the pitch transformed into lush communal gardens.

use. So, for example, 25 Cromwell Street in Gloucester and the school gymnasium at Dunblane were both razed to the ground.

Another theme emerging from this journey is one of reinvention. Many places featured in this book were built for one purpose, which then became redundant. Some were only ever intended for temporary use. More often than not, these places have reinvented themselves although frequently not without a long struggle. White City, the Millennium Dome and the Blackpool open-air baths are all examples of places whose original purpose disappeared, but which have found a new public purpose for a new age.

Some other places have been less successful at reinvention. Belle Vue in Manchester, for example, or Crystal Palace feel rather forlorn and wasted, despite many people's best efforts. This seems particularly true when what were once great places of public resort become anonymous housing estates or, more depressingly, anonymous retail parks as, for example, in the case of Burnden Park, Bolton.

Finally, there are those places that almost accidentally became the focus of attention – the café where the snail was found in the ginger beer or the hedge where the stolen World Cup was discovered. They are utterly ordinary and return to being so after the event, but they have demonstrated that, in the words of Sir Walter Scott, "...one crowded hour of glorious life is worth an age without a name."

There's no doubt that, in recent years, there's been an increased tendency to acknowledge and to commemorate the significance of places through the erection of plaques and memorials, and the marking of anniversaries. This recognition and this public acknowledgement of the importance of place are good in many ways. In another way, though, it's a shame because the charm, the fascination and the appeal of many of these places is that they are just there, or no longer there!

The discovery is the thing because what lies at the heart of this is the question to be asked in almost every street in the land, indeed across the planet: What was here before? What happened here? What happened next? May this journey continue!

BIBLIOGRAPHY

The Crystal Palace by Patrick Beaver, Hugh Evelyn Ltd (1977).

Crystal Palace Museum website: www.crystalpalacemuseum.org.uk

Crystal Palace Foundation website: www.crystalpalacefoundation.org.uk

Bromley in the Front Line by Lewis Blake, Bromley Libraries (2005).

A Very Ordinary Woman by Roland Gardner, on www.forces.stories.com

Historic Medway website: www.historicmedway.co.uk

Dunkirk by Sean Longden, Constable (2008).

English Heritage website: www.english-heritage.org.uk

What Happened After the Bomb by Nicholas Roe, *Daily Telegraph* (2000).

National Piers Society website: www.piers.co.uk

West Pier Trust website: www.westpier.co.uk

The Argus, Brighton: various articles.

The Tricorn; the Life and Death of a Sixties Icon by Celia Clark and Robert Cook, Tricorn Books (2009).

The Rubble Club website: www.therubbleclub.com

The News, Portsmouth: various articles.

UK Rock Festivals: www.ukrockfestivals.com

Wootton Bridge Historical Society website: www.woottonbridgeiow.co.uk

Forever Imber website: www.foreverimber.co.uk

World of Stuart website: www.worldofstuart.excellentcontent.com/imber

South Wales Echo: various articles.

Island Farm website: www.bracklaordnance.co.uk

Western Mail: various articles.

The First Four Minutes by Sir Roger Bannister, Sutton Publishing (2004).

Television Magazine of the Royal Television Society: various articles.

The Football Grounds of England and Wales by Simon Inglis, Willow Books (1983).

Highbury Square website: www.highburysquare.com

The Pirate Radio Hall of Fame website: www.offshoreradio.co.uk

Air Accidents Investigation Branch Report into the Kegworth Aircrash; Report 4/1990.

Kegworth Village website: www.kegworthvillage.com

National Horseracing Museum website: www.nhrm.co.uk

Lincolnshire Echo: various articles.

Butlins memories websites: www.bygonebutlins.com www.butlinsmemories.com

Bombardment – the Day the East Coast Bled by Mark Marsay, Great Northern Publishing (1999).

Scarborough Maritime Heritage website: www.scarboroughsmaritimeheritage.org.uk

Middlesbrough Evening Gazette: various articles.

Ayresome Park website: www.ayresomepark.co.uk

Sunderland Maritime Heritage website: ww.sunderlandmaritimeheritage.co.uk

Newcastle Community Heritage website: www.newcastlecommunityheritage.org

Elephant House Café website: www.elephanthouse.biz

Maritime and Coastguard Agency website: www.mcga.gov.uk

Scapa Flow website: www.scapaflow.co.uk

Gazeteer of Scotland website: www.scottish-places.info

Highland Council website: www.highland.gov.uk

Dunblane Centre website: www.dunblanecentre.co.uk

Faculty of Advocates website: www.advocates.org.uk

Paisley Express: various articles.

Dryfesdale Lodge website: www.dryfesdalelodge.co.uk

'Lockerbie Wreckage Sold', article in *The People*, December 2008.

Mardale Green website: www.mardalegreentalk.net

Donald Campbell, Bluebird and the Final Record Attempt by Neil Sheppard, The History Press (2011).

Carnforth Station website: www.carnforthstation.co.uk

The Worldwide Guide to Movie Locations by Tony Reeves, Titan Books (2001).

Lidos website: www.lidos.org.uk

Motorways website: www.cbrd.co.uk

Lancashire County Council website: www.lancashire.gov.uk

Motorway Archive Trust: www.ukmotorwayarchive.org

Football ground website: www.footballgroundguide.com

The History of the Haçienda by Dave Haslam, for the Pride of Manchester (2003).

'Inside Shipman's Surgery', *Mail On Sunday* article, by Lucy Laing and Jo Knowsley (2001).

Waverley Orgreave Community website: www.waverleycommunity.org.uk

Old Swan Hotel website: www.classiclodges.co.uk/oldswan

Yeadon Above The Rest by Kenneth Cothliff, Croft Publications (2011).

Mother Worked at Avro by Gerald Myers, Compaif Graphics (1995).

Bradford Telegraph and Argus: various articles.

Wharfedale Observer: various articles.

Return to the House of Evil by David Hudson and Terry O'Hanlon, *Sunday Mirror* (2005).

Belle Vue website: www.manchesterhistory.net

The Bolton News: various articles www.theboltonnews.co.uk

Trafford General Hospital website: www.trafford.nhs.uk

The Liverpool Overhead Railway by Charles E. Box, revised by Adrian Jarvis, Ian Allan (1984).

Riverside Drive, Liverpool community website: www.riversidedrive.org.uk

Liverpool Daily Post: various articles.

Cavern Club website: www.cavernclub.org

Wirral local history website: www.oldwirral.com

Birmingham Mail: various articles.

Sunday Mercury: various articles.

Horton's Birmingham website: www.hortons.co.uk

Birmingham architecture website: www.birminghamroundabout.co.uk

Pebble Mill website: www.pebblemill.org

Not Forgotten, the 1939 IRA Bomb Attack by Simon Shaw at Coventry local history website: www.historiccoventry.co.uk

Airship Heritage Trust website: www.airshipsonline.com

Cliveden House Hotel: www.clivedenhouse.co.uk and National Trust website: www.nationaltrust.org.uk/cliveden

Southbank centre website: www.southbankcentre.co.uk

Theatres Trust website: www.theatrestrust.org.uk

How Pickles the Dog Dug Up the Accursed World Cup by Paul Fleckney (2006) on www.thisislocallondon.co.uk

Epsom local history website: www.epsomandewellhistoryexplorer.org.uk

Brooklands Museum website: www.brooklandsmuseum.com

Farnborough Air Sciences Trust website: www.airsciences.org.uk

'Haunted by Hungerford' by Natasha Courtenay-Smith, *Daily Mail* (2007); 'The Minute that Ruined My Life' by Simon Trump, *Daily Mail* (2008)

Slapton Sands memorial website: www.shermantank.co.uk

'Oil Spills – Legacy of the Torrey Canyon' by Patrick Barkham, *The Guardian* (2010).

Marconi Centre, Poldhu website: www.marconi-centre-poldhu.org.uk

Bristol Filton Airport website: www.bristolfilton.co.uk

Save Filton Airfield campaign website: www.savefiltonairfield.org

Bristol Evening Post: various articles.

Concorde website: www.concordesst.com

Greenham Business Park website: www.greenham-business-park.co.uk

That Woman – The Life of Wallis Simpson, Duchess of Windsor by Anne Serba, Weidenfeld & Nicolson (2011).

Grunwick dispute, Leeds University website: www.leeds.ac.uk/strikingwomen

The History of Broadcasting in the United Kingdom by Asa Briggs, Oxford University Press (1961).

The First London Olympics 1908 by Rebecca Jenkins, Piatkus Books (2008).

Never Had It So Good – A History of Britain from Suez to The Beatles by Dominic Sandbrook, Little, Brown (2005).

BBC News website: various articles.

The Guardian website: various articles.

The Independent website: various articles.

Daily Telegraph website: various articles.

Daily Mail website: various articles.

London Evening Standard: various articles.

Urban Explorers website: www.28dayslater.co.uk

INDEX

ACKNOWLEDGMENTS

My thanks for the help and assistance provided by:
Ken Kiss, Melvyn Harrison, John Chambers, Cindy O'Halloran, Rowena Willard-Wright, Andrew Mosley, Richard Baker, Rachel Clark, Gail Beard, Celia Clark, Roy Murphy, Ruth Underwood, Tony Moran, Ian Tabor, Liam Ronan, Gillian Thomas, Karen Crandon, David Davies, Marcus Grodentz, Kate Nelmes, Andy John, John Trenouth, Josephine Olley, Ian Cook, Linda Vickers, Liz Bruce, Simon Schaffer, Sheila Sharp, Charlie Partridge, Sharon Edwards, Lesley Penniston, Roger Billington, Carol Longbone, Angela Kale, Graham Bell, Sheila Jones, Clive Goodwin, Jude Callister, Gordon Fyfe, Steve Birnie, Lesley Shaw, Susan McIver, John Gair, Geoff Carroll, Adam Simmons, John Adams, Tony Sharkey, Mike Warren, Harry Yeadon, Mike Woodcock, Alison Whelan, Neil Anderson, Trevor Braithwait, Tim Love, Gerald Myers, Kenneth Cothliff, Ian Priestley, Caroline Walker, Perry Austin-Clarke, Lesley Holland, Emer Scott, Jimmy Wagg, Eamonn O'Neill, Keith Thornton, Jon Keats, Rebecca Holden, Cathy Elwin, Barry Gregory, Sharon Brown, Kim Barnes, Amy Dixon, Tony Rose, Andre Bremermann, Di McDonald, Peter Burt, Dawn Rothwell, Julian May, Andrew Commons, Justine Eves, Hayley O'Keefe, Patricia O'Connor, Toby Porter, Ricky Allen, Angela Turney, Allan Winn, Graham Rood, Claire Barnes, Peter Roper, Alan Hale, Jean Foxwell, Keith Matthew, Mitchell Dugan, Jamie Ritchie, Kate McLean, Mark Bezodis, Nima Poovaya-Smith and anyone else whom I have inadvertently overlooked.

My particular thanks to my former colleagues at the National Media Museum, the National Railway Museum and the Science Museum:- Caroline Dempsey, Ruth Kitchin, Brian Liddy, Toni Booth, Jonathan Newby, Paul Goodman, Iain Baird, Colin Harding, Helen Sunderland and Ed Bartholomew.

My special thanks to Martin Stephens, Colin Panter and Dave McCloughlin (PA Images for helping facilitate the book), to John Stachiewicz, Steve Abbott and Paul Richards (for advice and support); to Edward Stourton (for kindly writing a foreword); to Barbara Philpott (for practical help); and, above all, to Hilary Philpott (for practical help, encouragement, understanding and unfailing support).

I would like to dedicate this book to my Dad, Brian Philpott, who loved visiting places like these.

PICTURE CREDITS